Butterfly Coloring Book

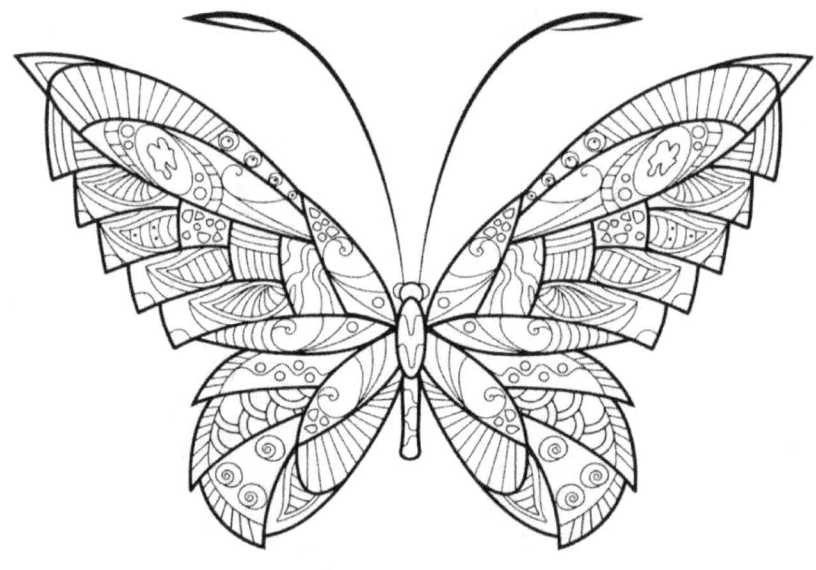

Copyright © 2019 by Jonathan Rockwell

All rights reserved. No part of this publication may be reproduced, distributed, or transmitted in any form or by any means, including photocopying, recording, or other electronic or mechanical methods.

10 Fascinating Butterfly facts

1. There are more than 17,500 recorded butterfly species around the world, 750 of which can be found in the U.S.

2. Butterflies and moths are part of the class of insects in the order Lepidoptera. Butterflies are flying insects with large scaly wings. Like all insects, they have six jointed legs and three body parts: the head, the thorax and the abdomen. The wings are attached to the thorax and they also have a pair of antennae, compound eyes and an exoskeleton.

3. The Cabbage White, seen above, is the most common butterfly in the U.S. Although it appears mostly white with black markings on the top of its wings, underneath those wings are yellowish-green. These butterflies have a wing spread of just about two inches. Males have only one spot on each wing, while females have two. As you probably know, you can find Cabbage Whites in most open spaces, including gardens, roadsides, parks and cities.

4. Monarch butterflies migrate to get away from the cold. However, they are the only insect that migrates an average of 2,500 miles to find a warmer climate. The iconic North American Monarch has been greatly affected by extreme weather events, going through drastic dips and spikes in numbers over the past several decades. The overall pattern continues to point downward, with a 95 percent population decline over the last 20 years, but conservation efforts are helping:

5. Monarchs are not the only butterfly that migrate. The Painted Lady, American Lady, Red Admiral, Cloudless Sulphur, Skipper, Sachem, Question Mark, Clouded Skipper, Fiery Skipper and Mourning Cloak are among the other butterflies that also migrate, but not as far as the Monarchs.

6. The Common Buckeye Butterfly is one of the most striking butterflies, with its bold multicolored eyespots and thick upper-wing bars, all designed to frighten away any birds that might be tempted to chomp on them. If you look under its wings, you'll find a more abstract profusion of brown, orange and beige. These insects are pretty common all over North and Central America, although you won't find them in the Pacific Northwest or in the far north of Canada.

7. The Orange Barred Sulphur Butterfly is one that you can find all over the Americas and the Caribbean. It's very distinctive, being bright yellow with patches of orange marking both forewings and hindwings. Females tend to be bigger and darker than their male counterparts and unusually, just like the adult butterflies, the caterpillars also have bright yellow bodies segmented by dark stripes.

8. Speaking of caterpillars, how much do you know about the life cycle of a butterfly? The butterfly starts its life as an egg, laid on a leaf. The caterpillar (larva) hatches from the egg and eats leaves or flowers. It loses its skin many times as it grows, increasing greatly in size. Eventually it turns into a pupa, or chrysalis and finally a beautiful adult butterfly emerges and the cycle continues.

9. An adult butterfly has a very short life: just three to four weeks. However, the entire life cycle of a butterfly can range between 2 and 8 months, depending on the species. Some migratory butterflies, such as the North American Monarch, can live as long as 7 to 8 months in one generation.

10. The Giant Swallowtail Butterfly, as its name implies, is one of the biggest butterflies, with a wing spread of four to seven inches. The female is once again bigger than the male. It too is found throughout North America and sometimes as far south as South America. These butterflies are called "swallow" because they have long tails on their hind wings that resemble the long, pointed tails of the birds known as swallows.

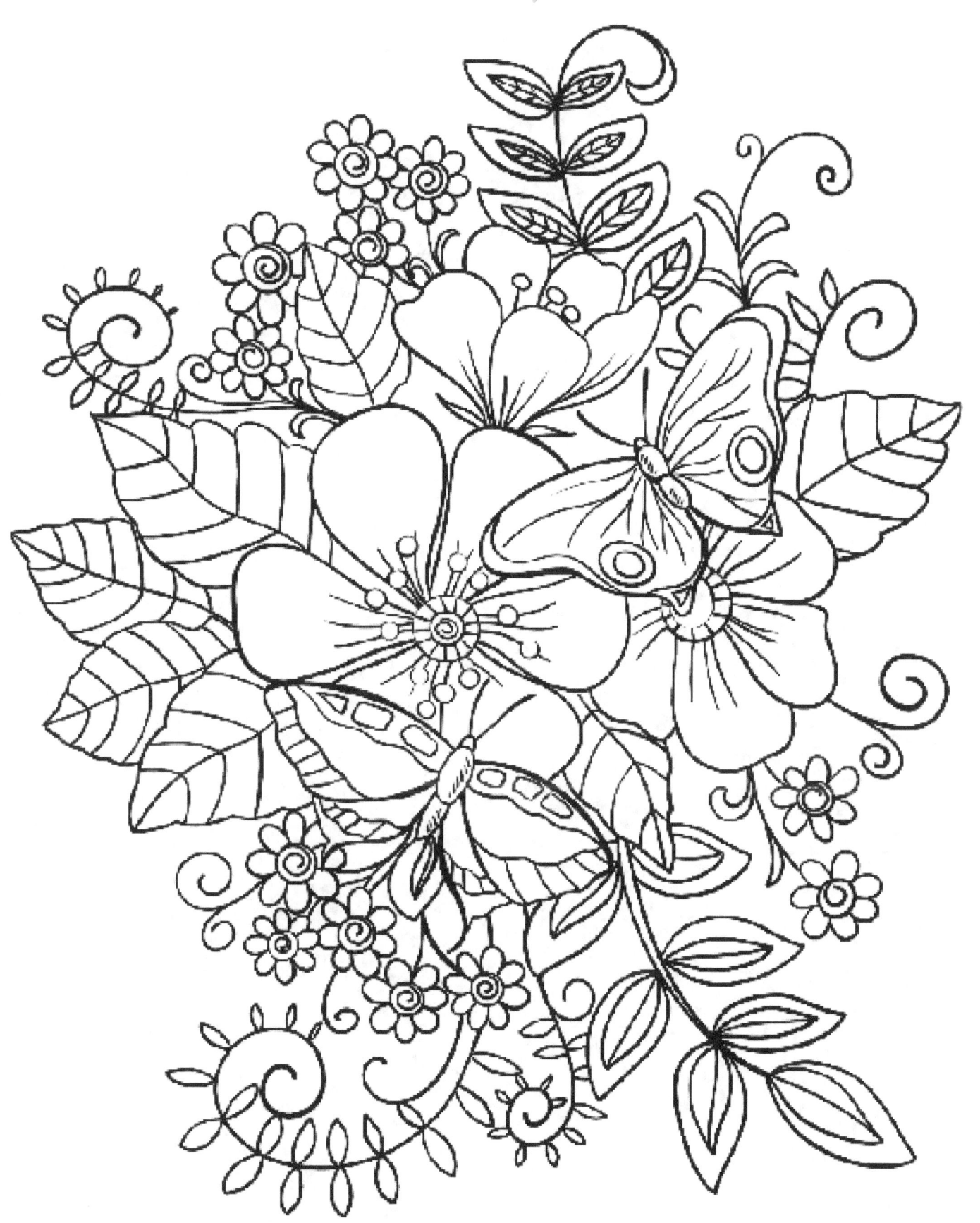

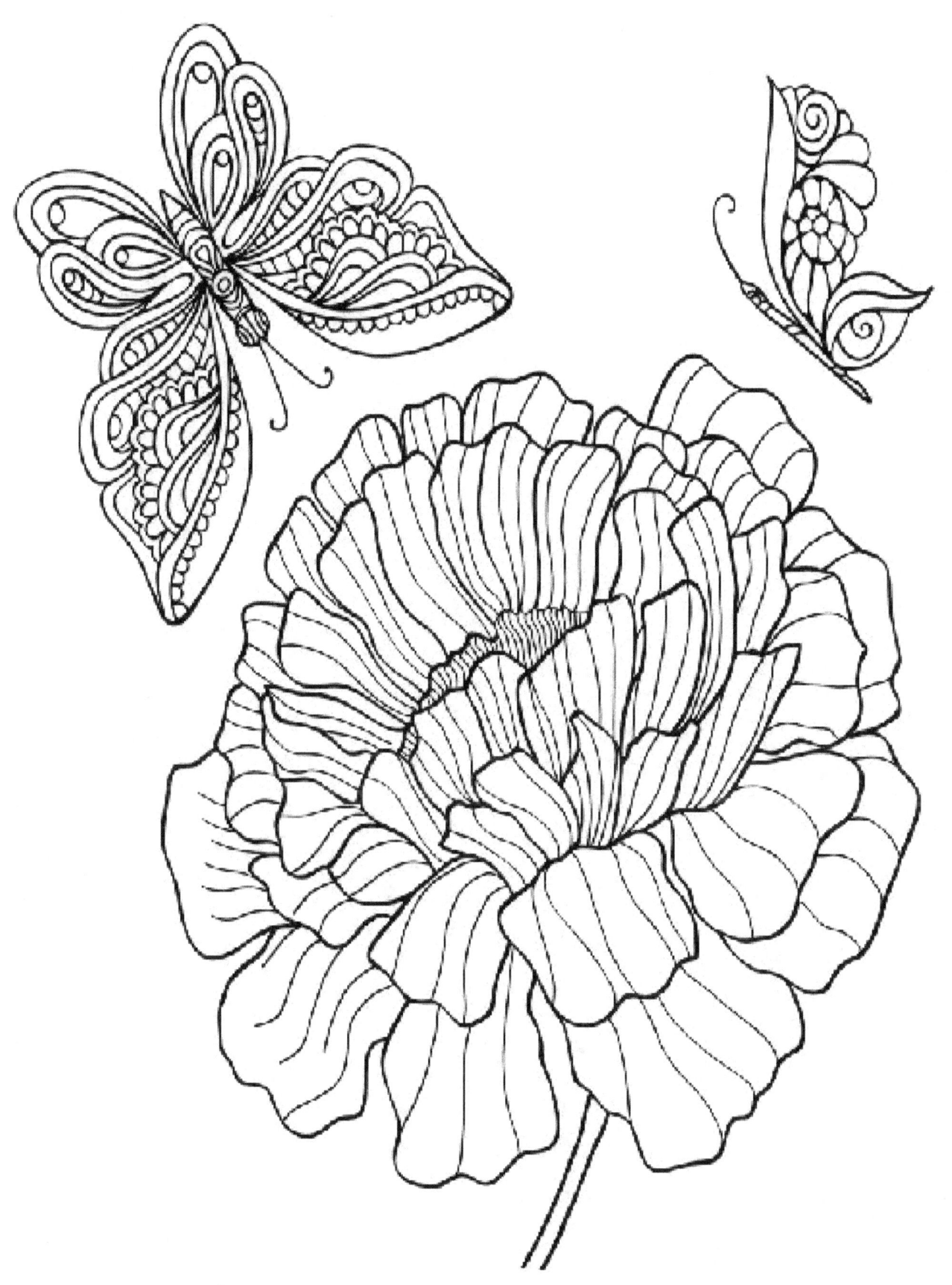

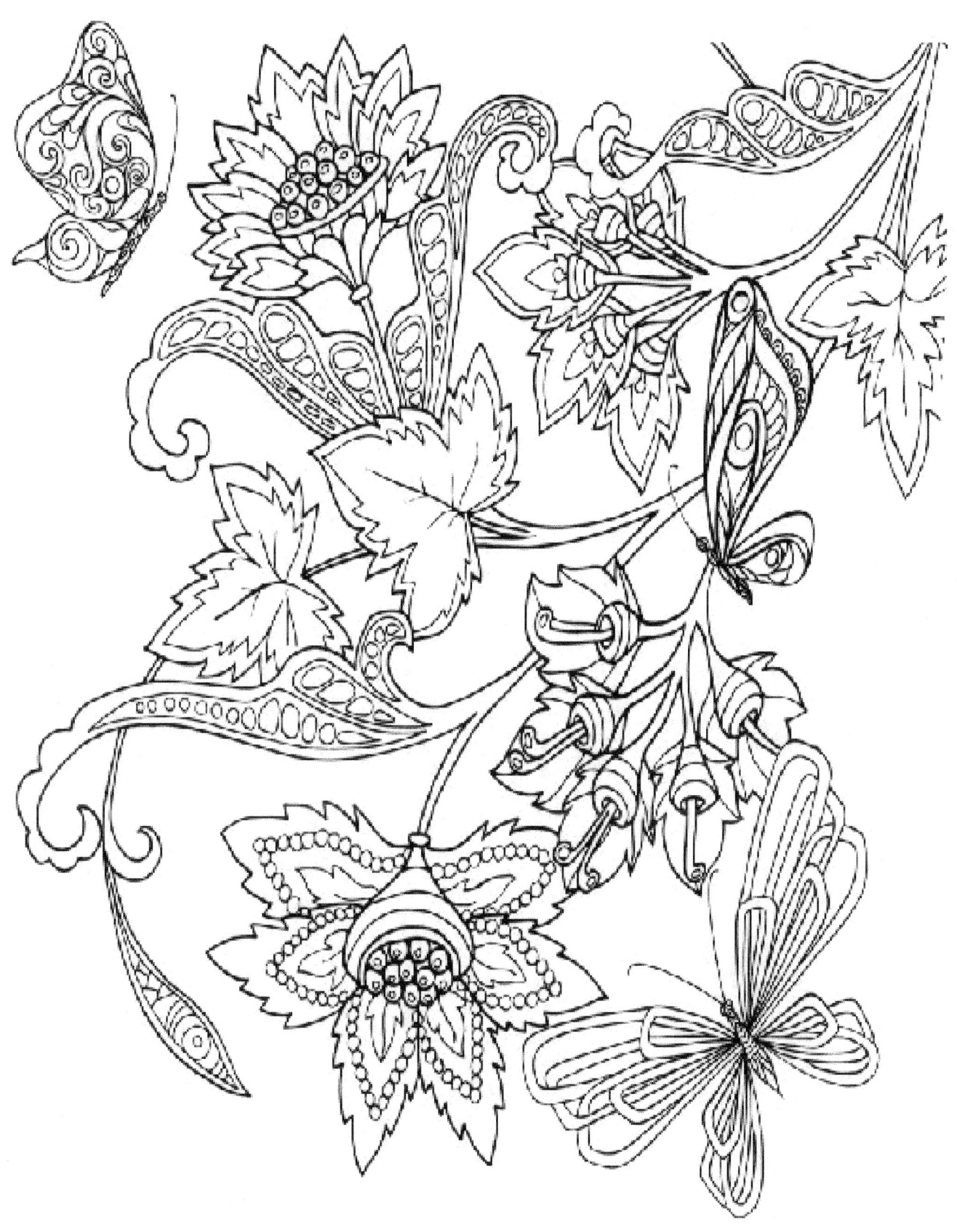

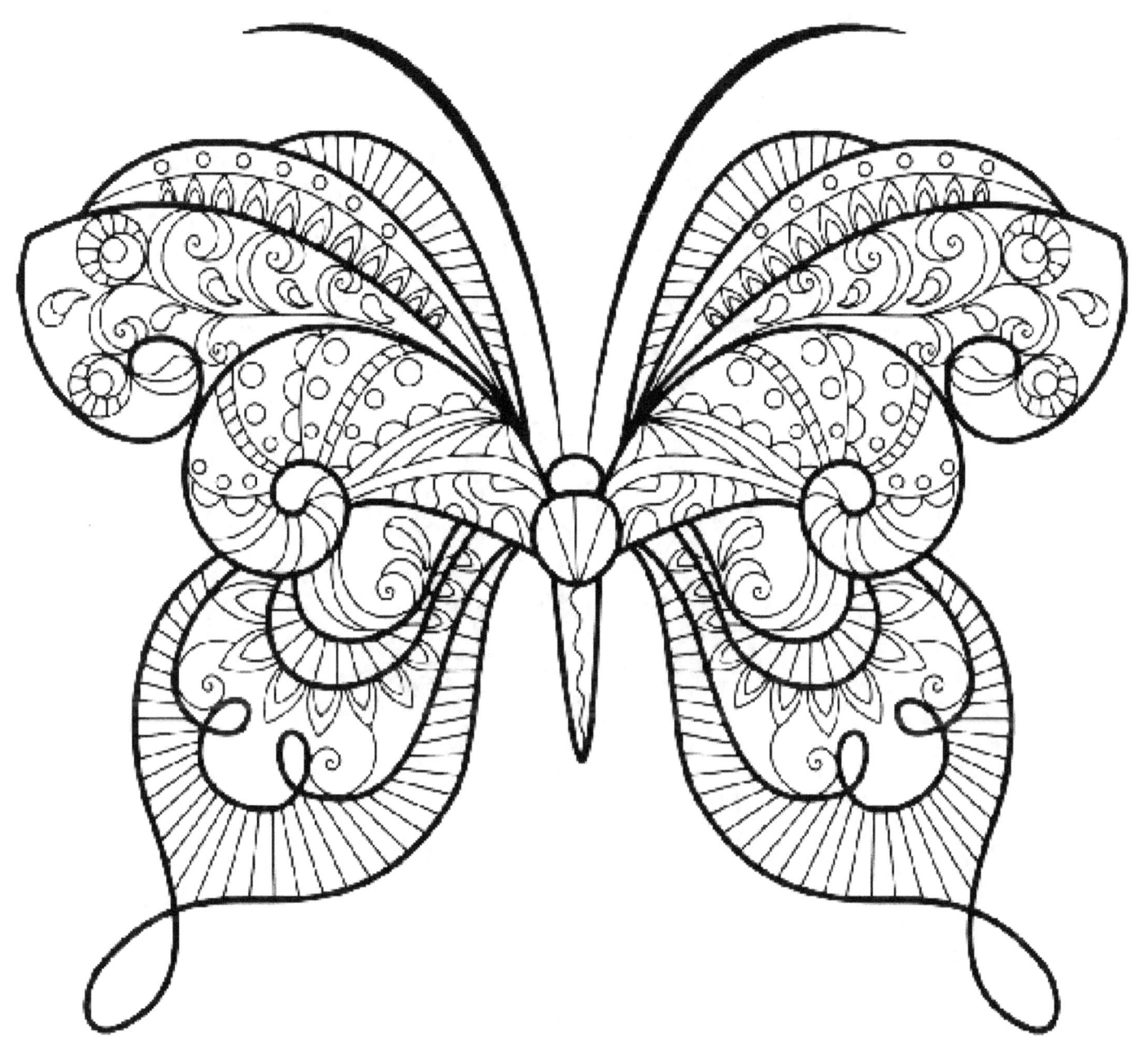

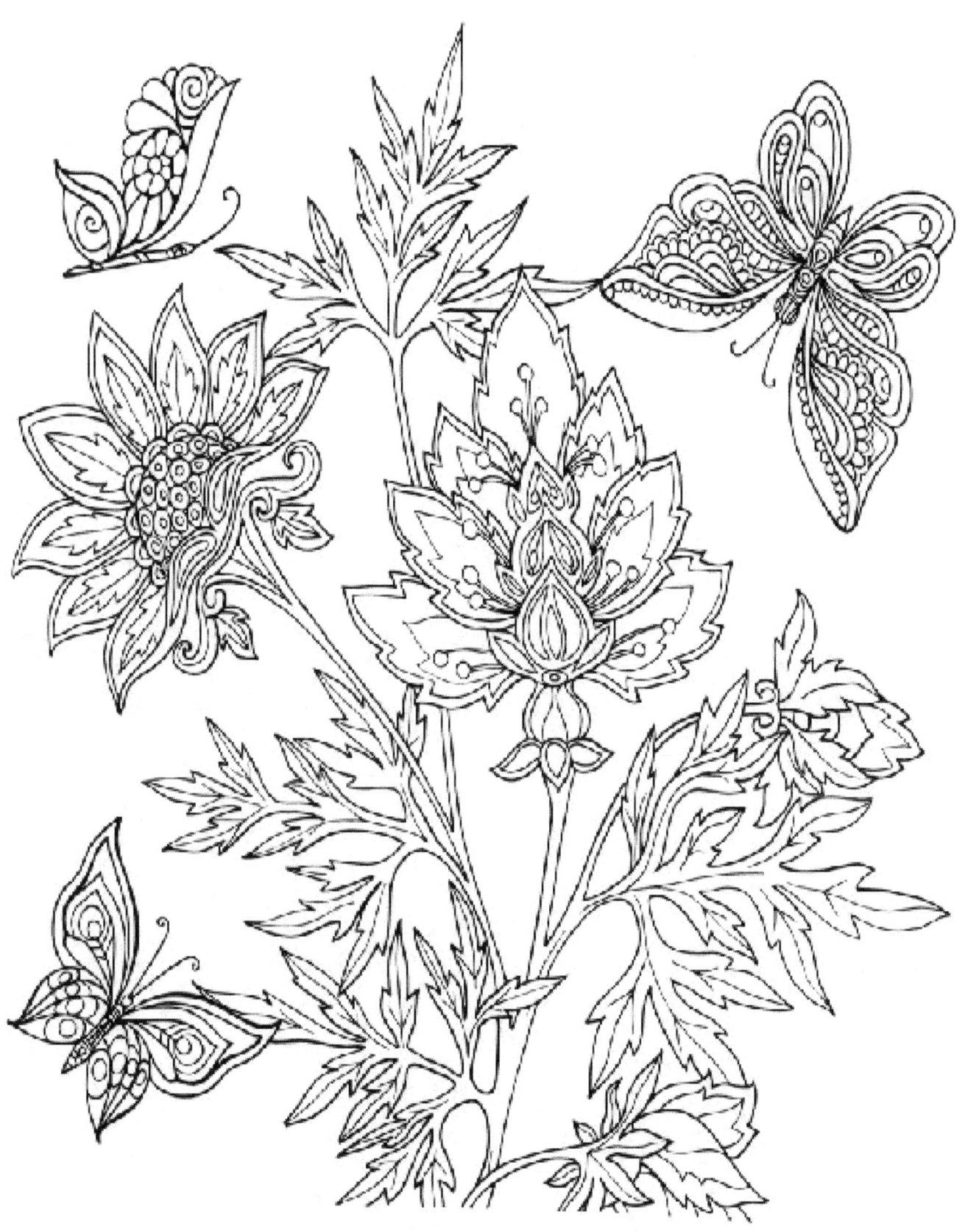

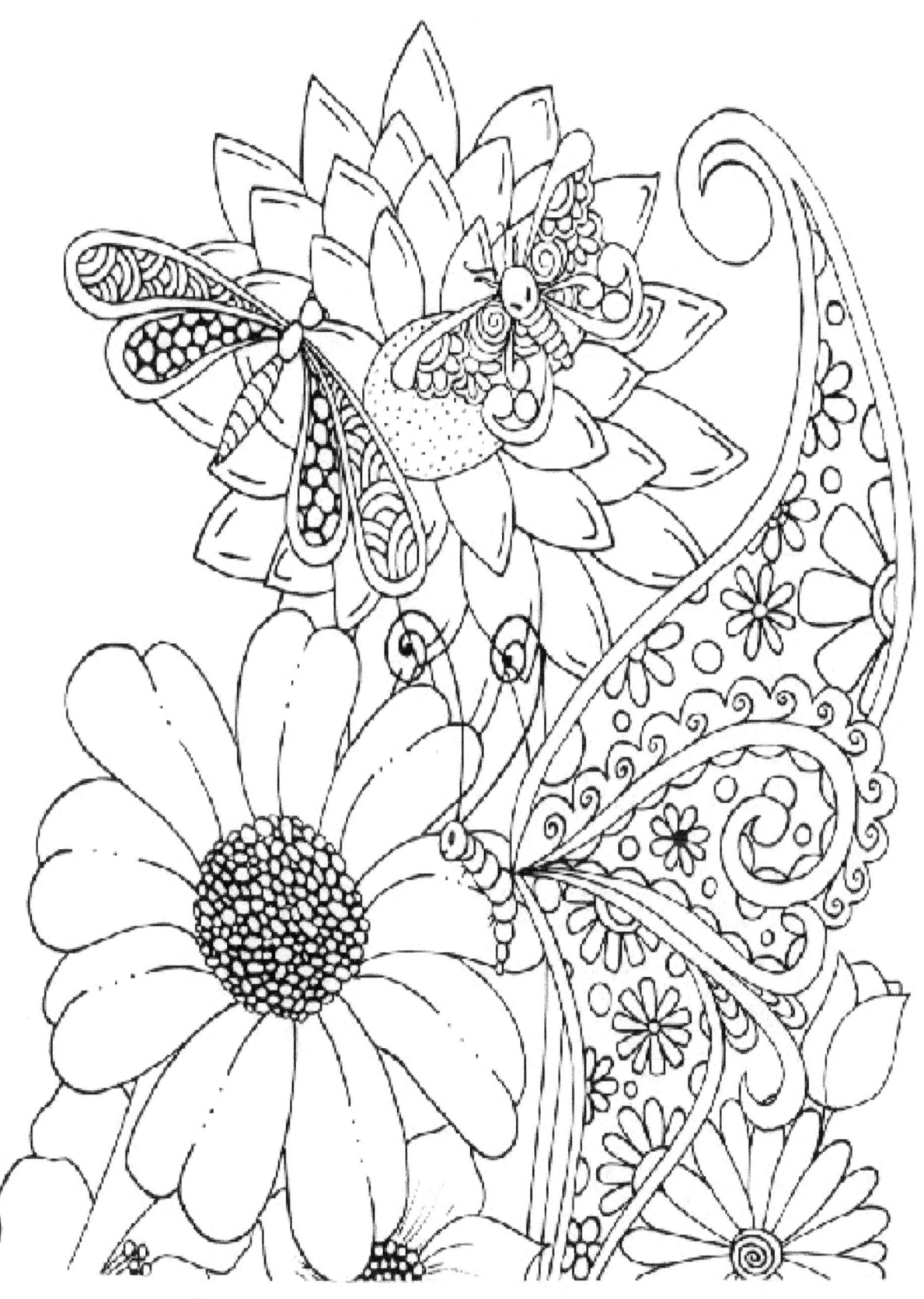

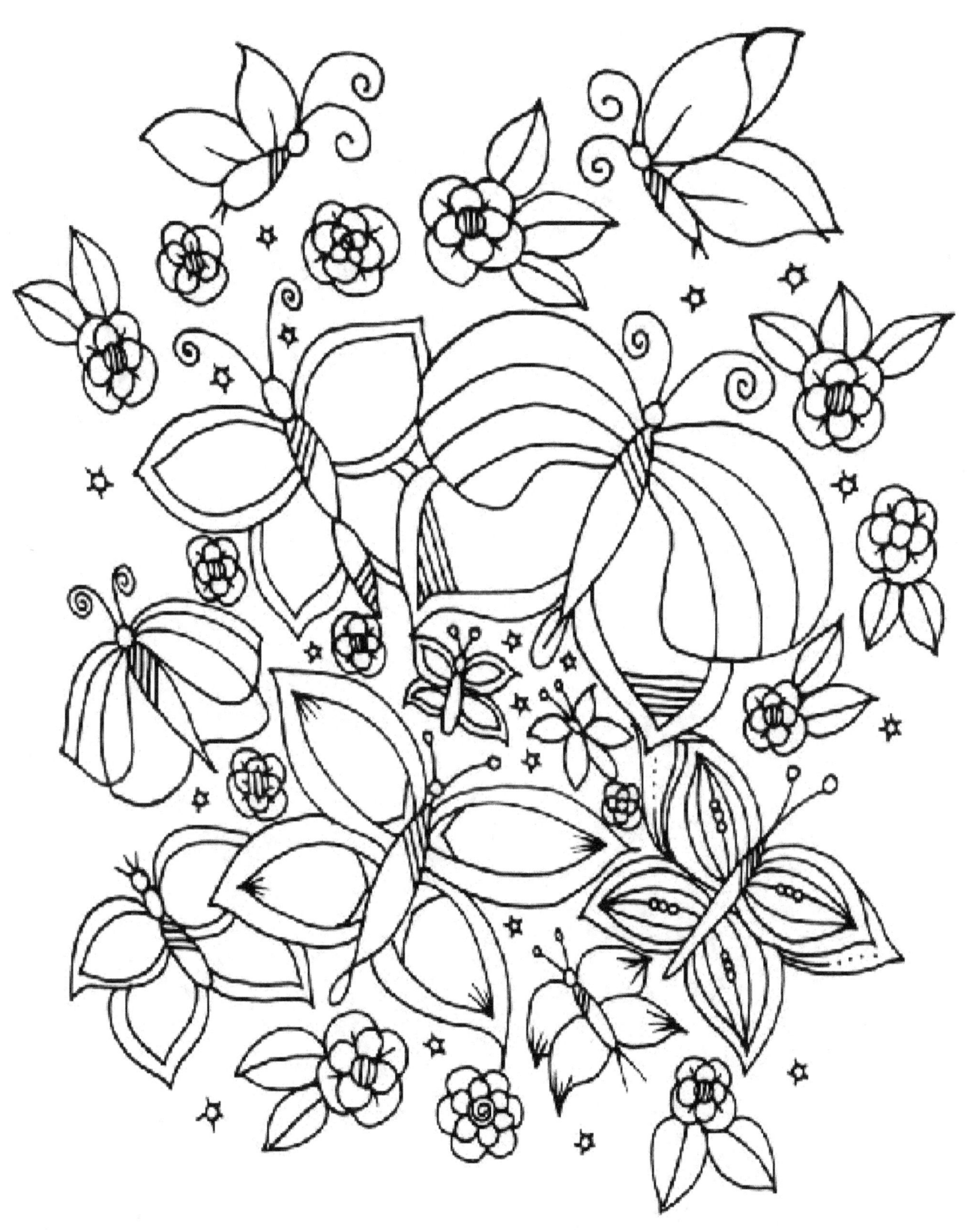

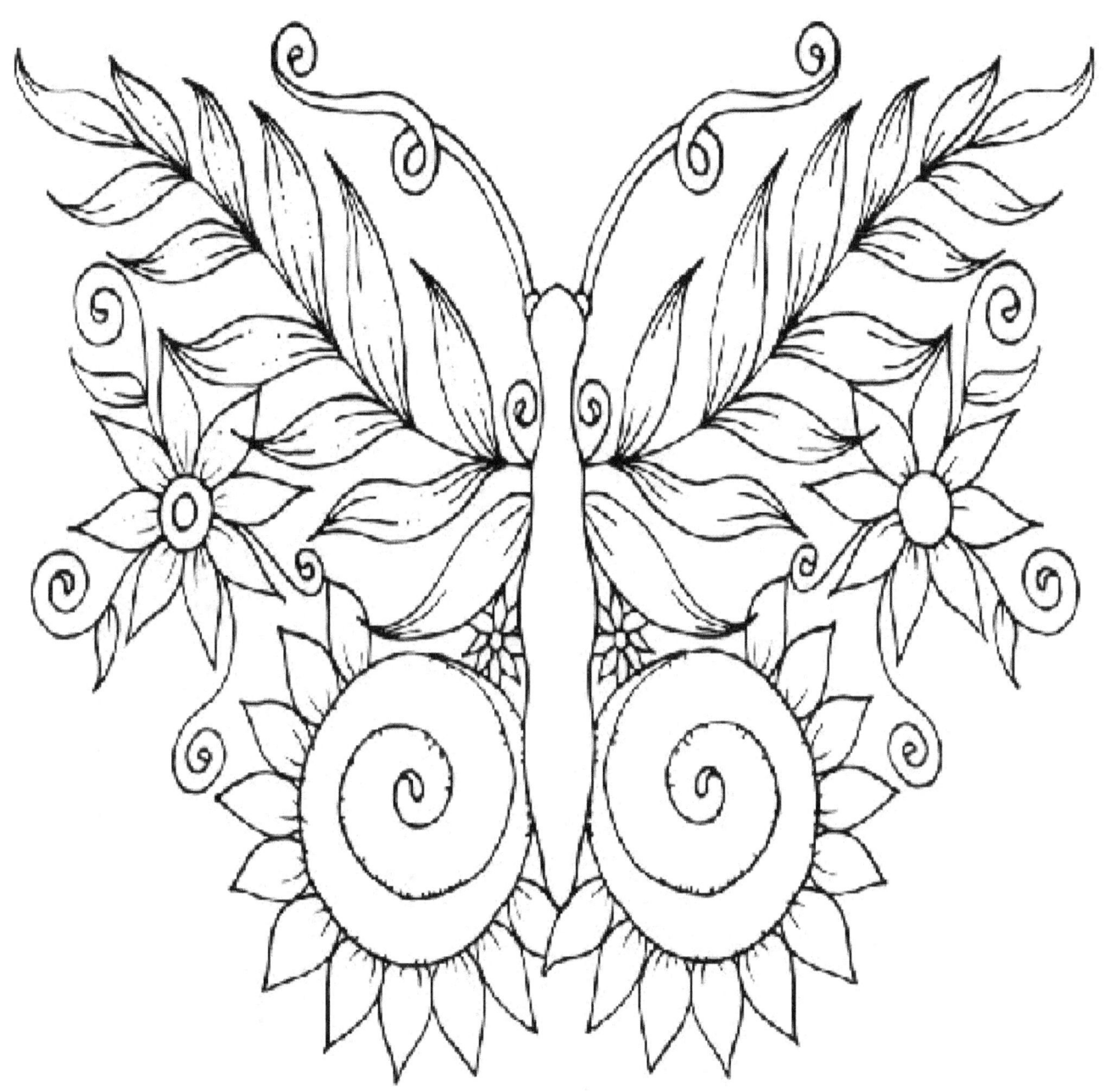

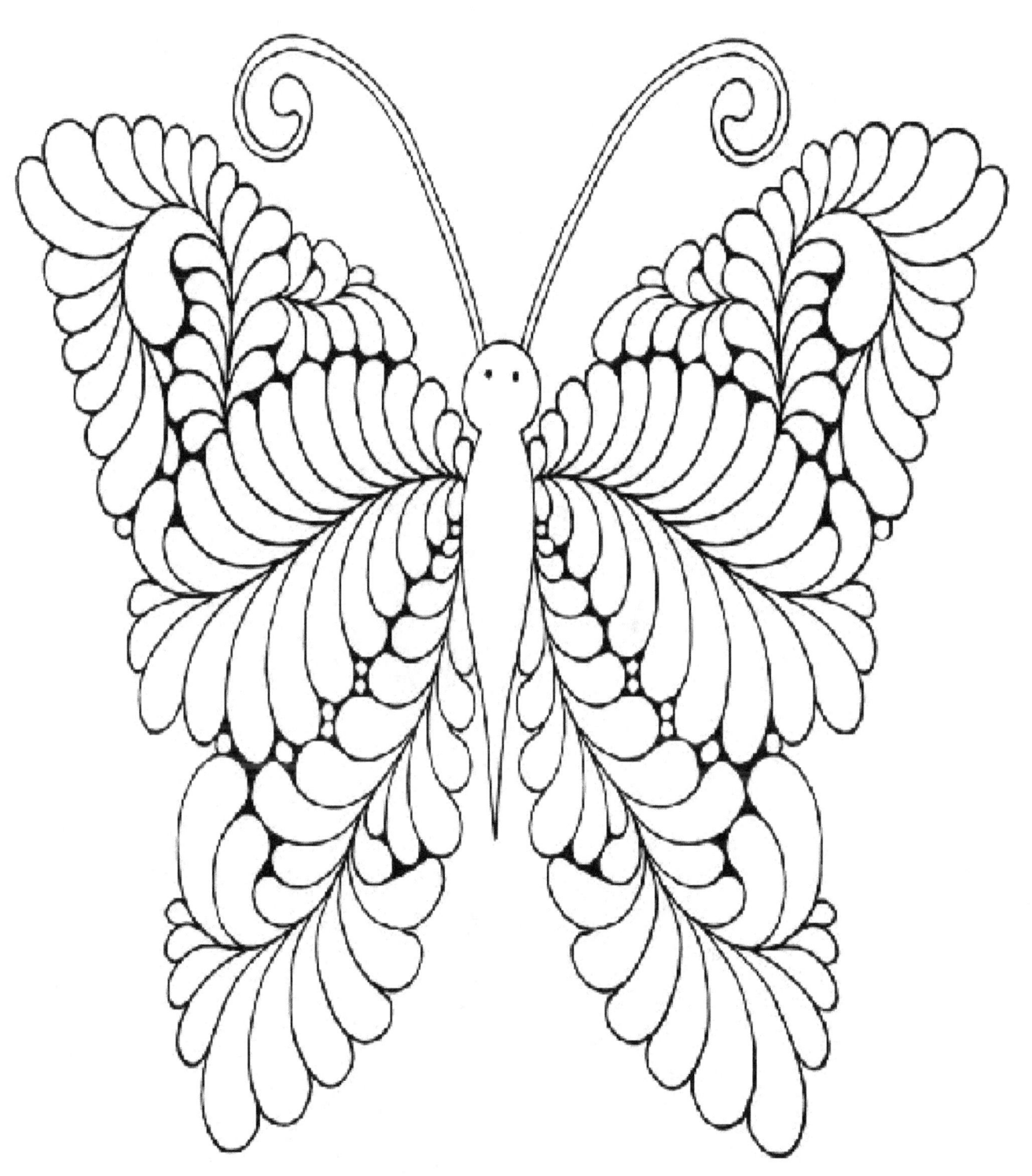

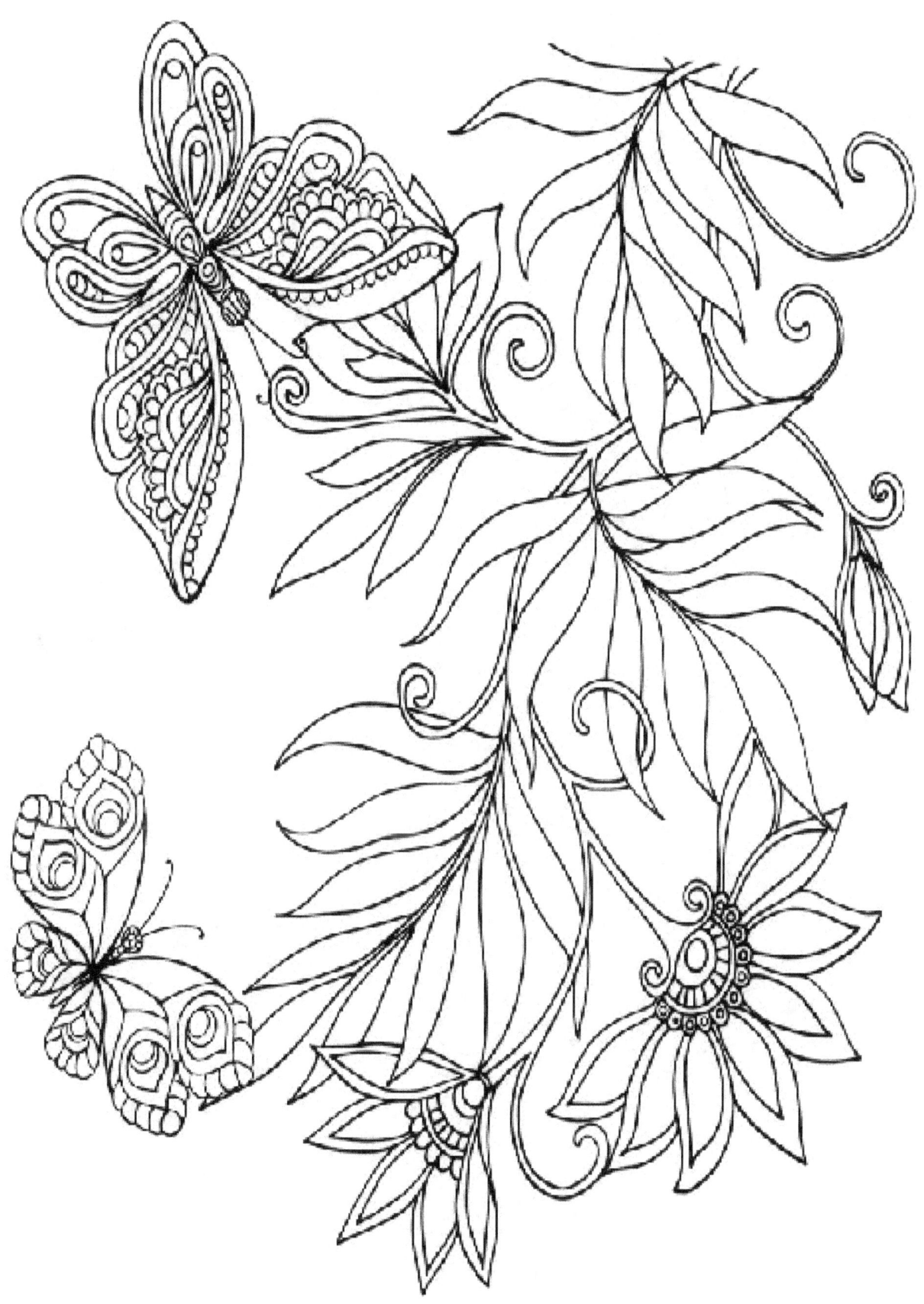

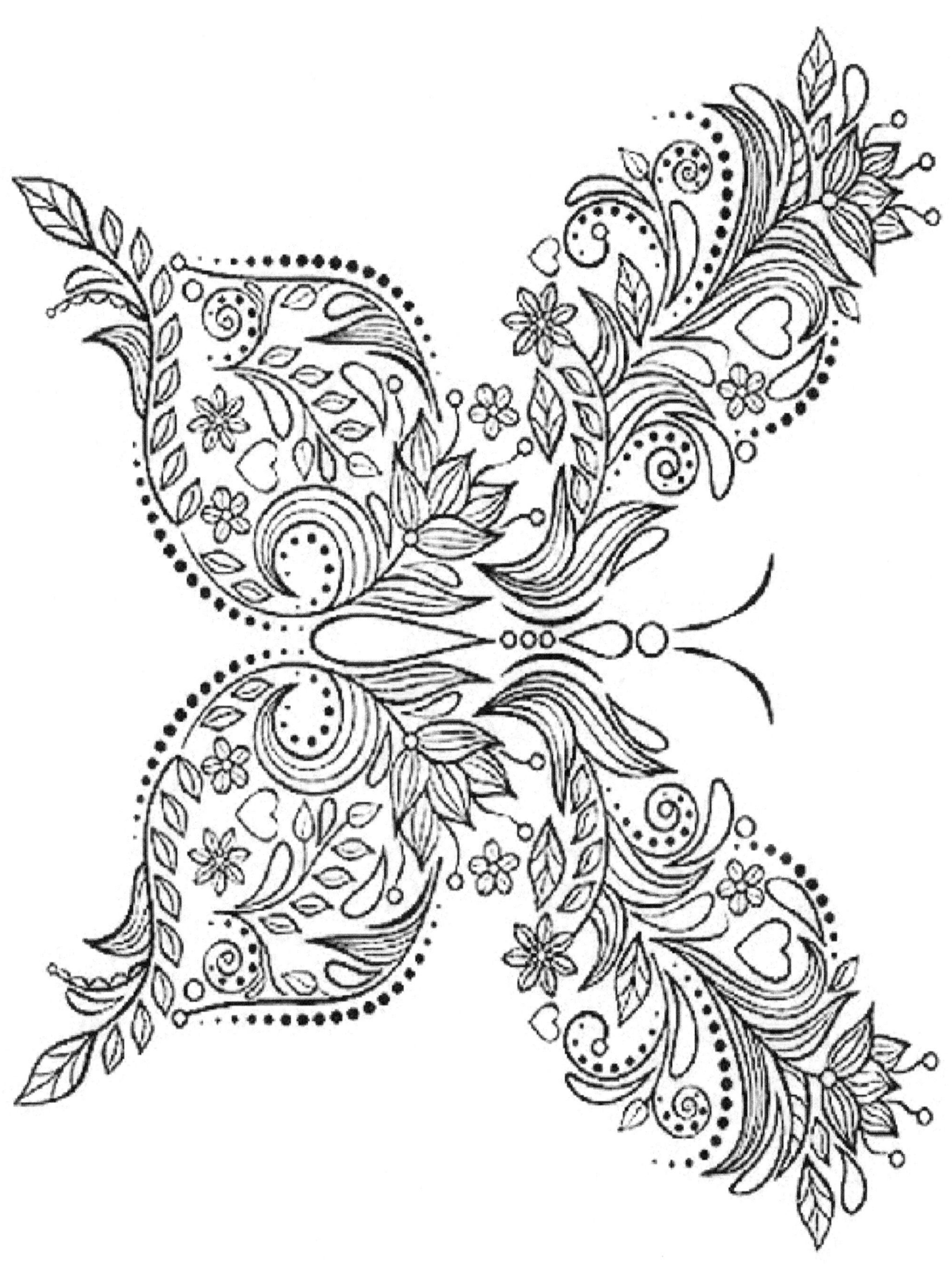

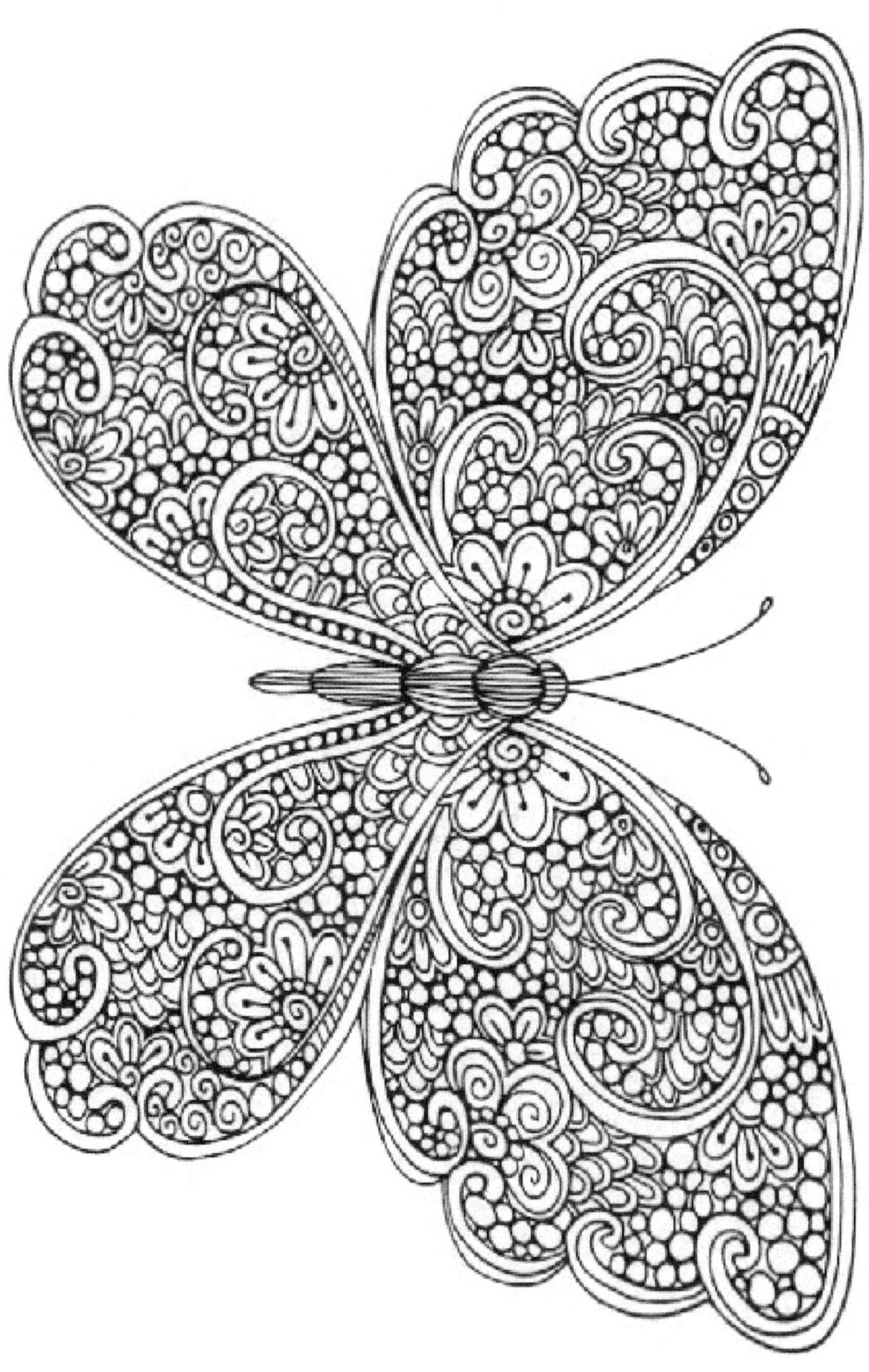

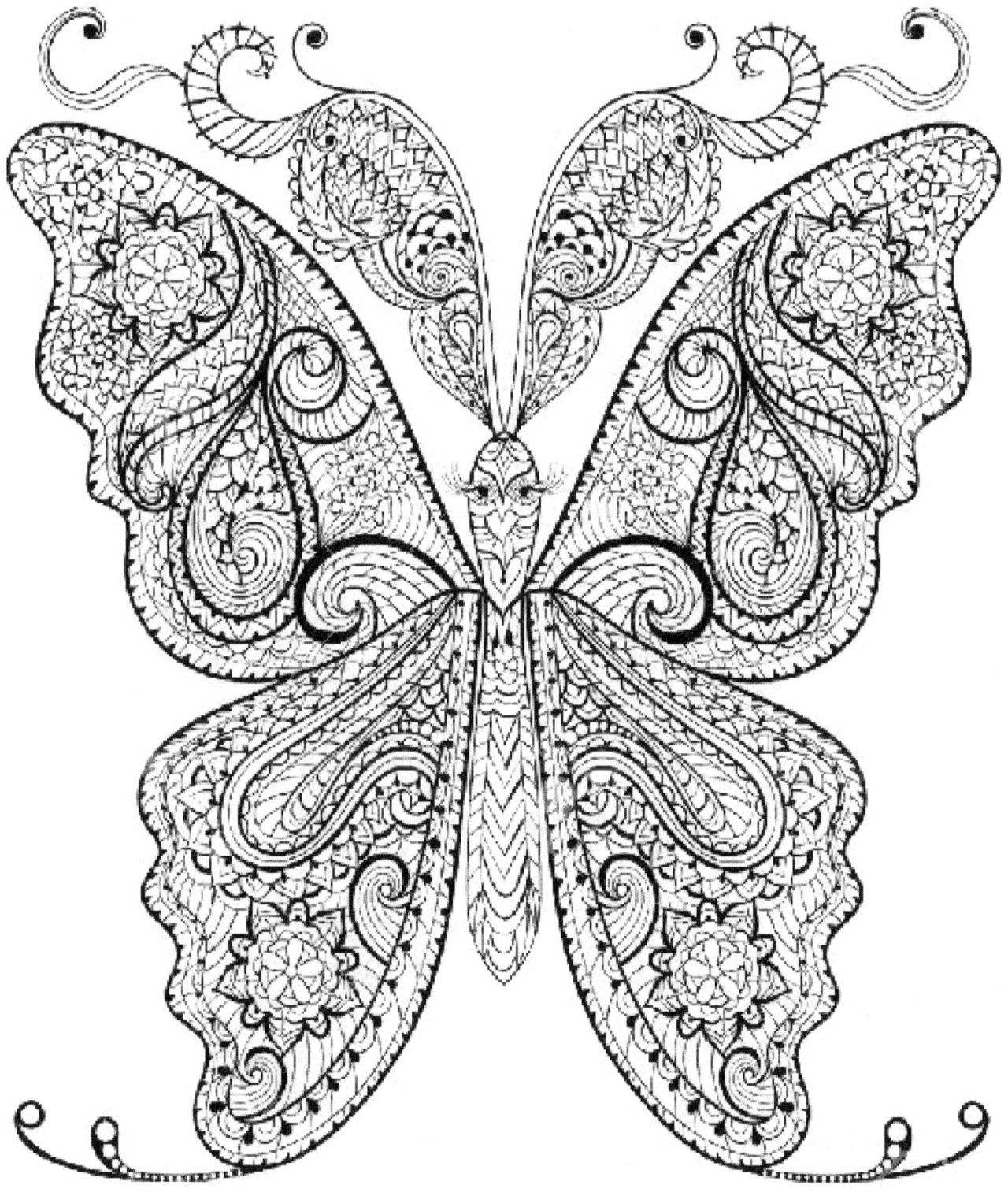

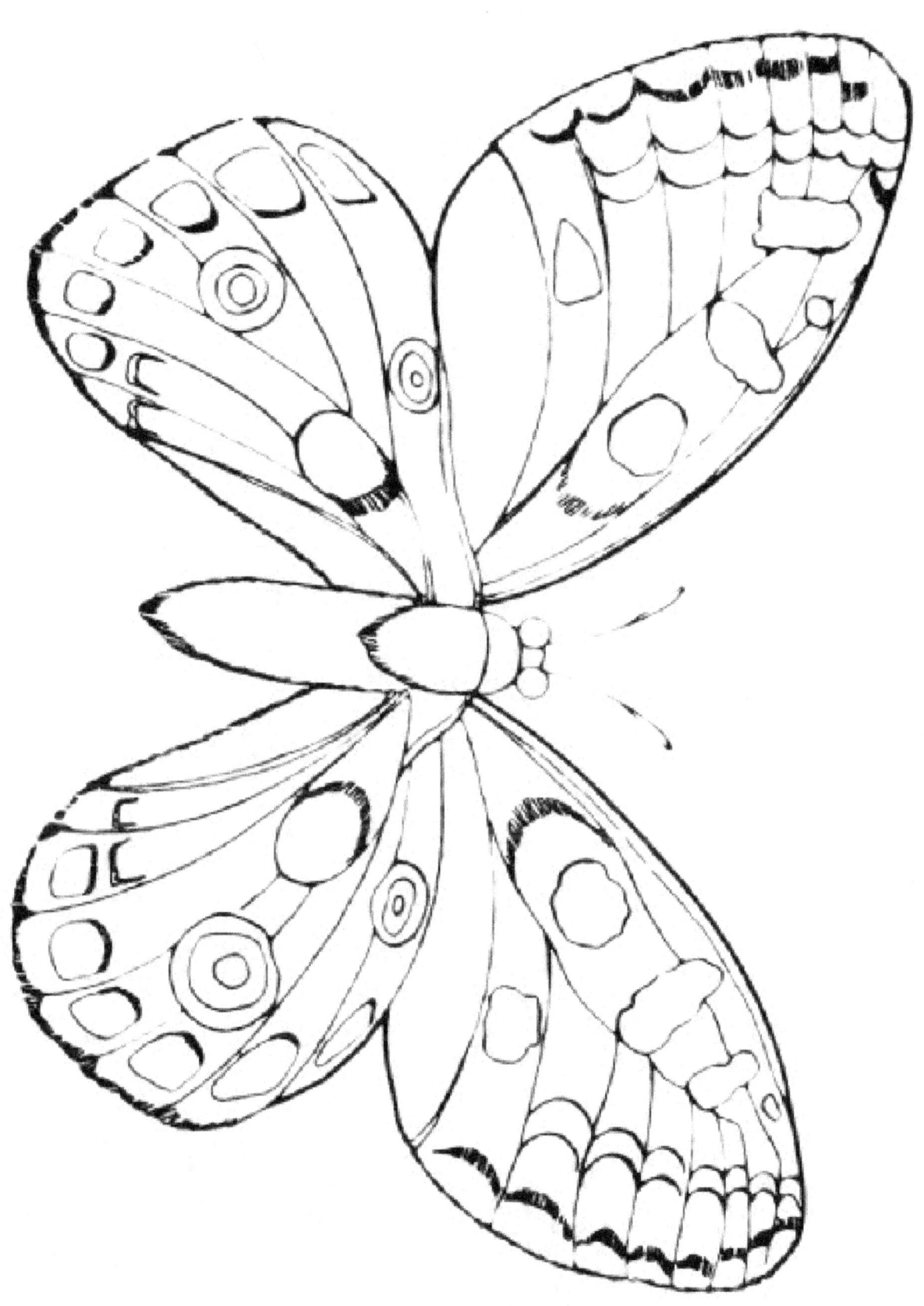

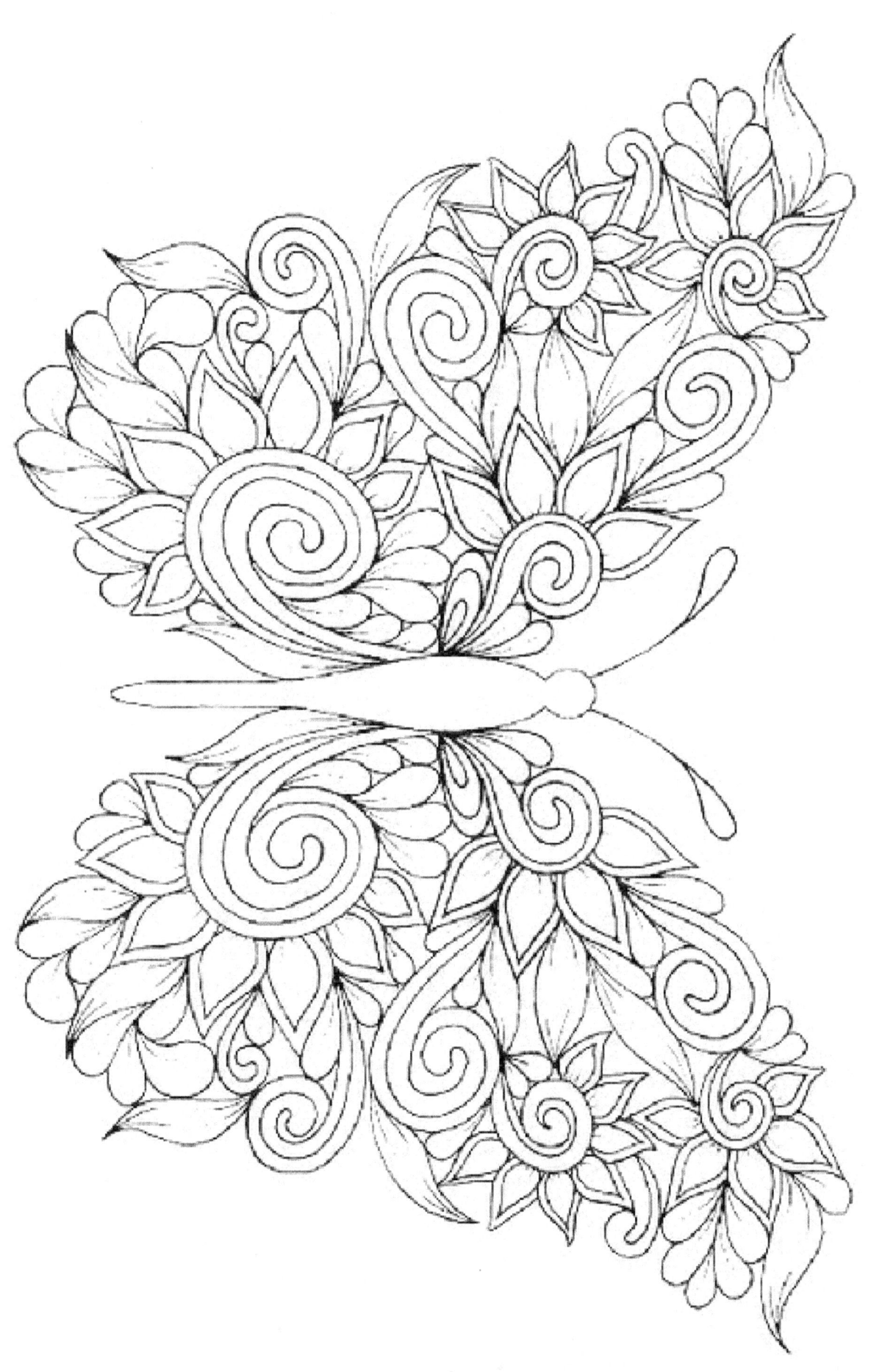

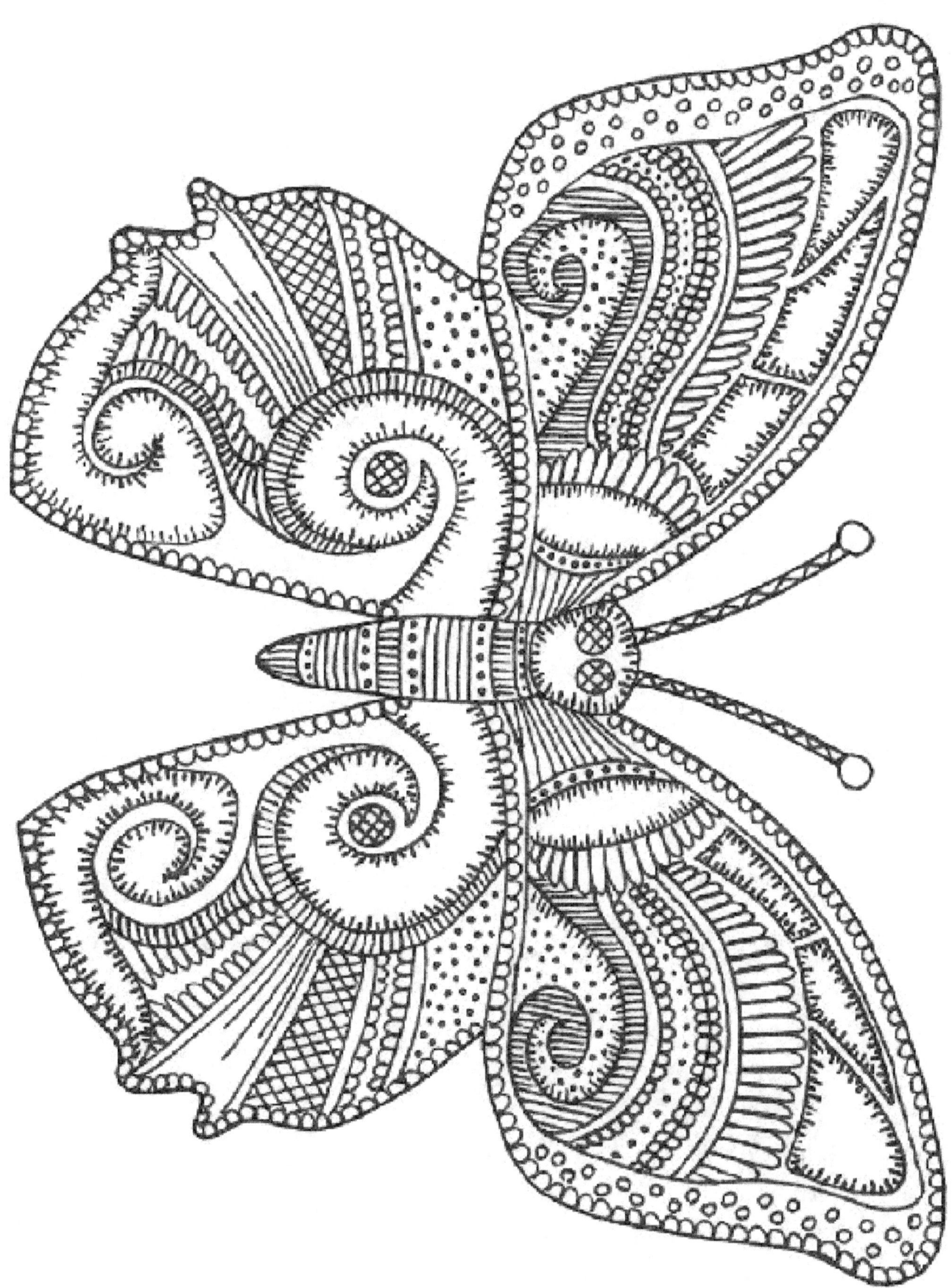

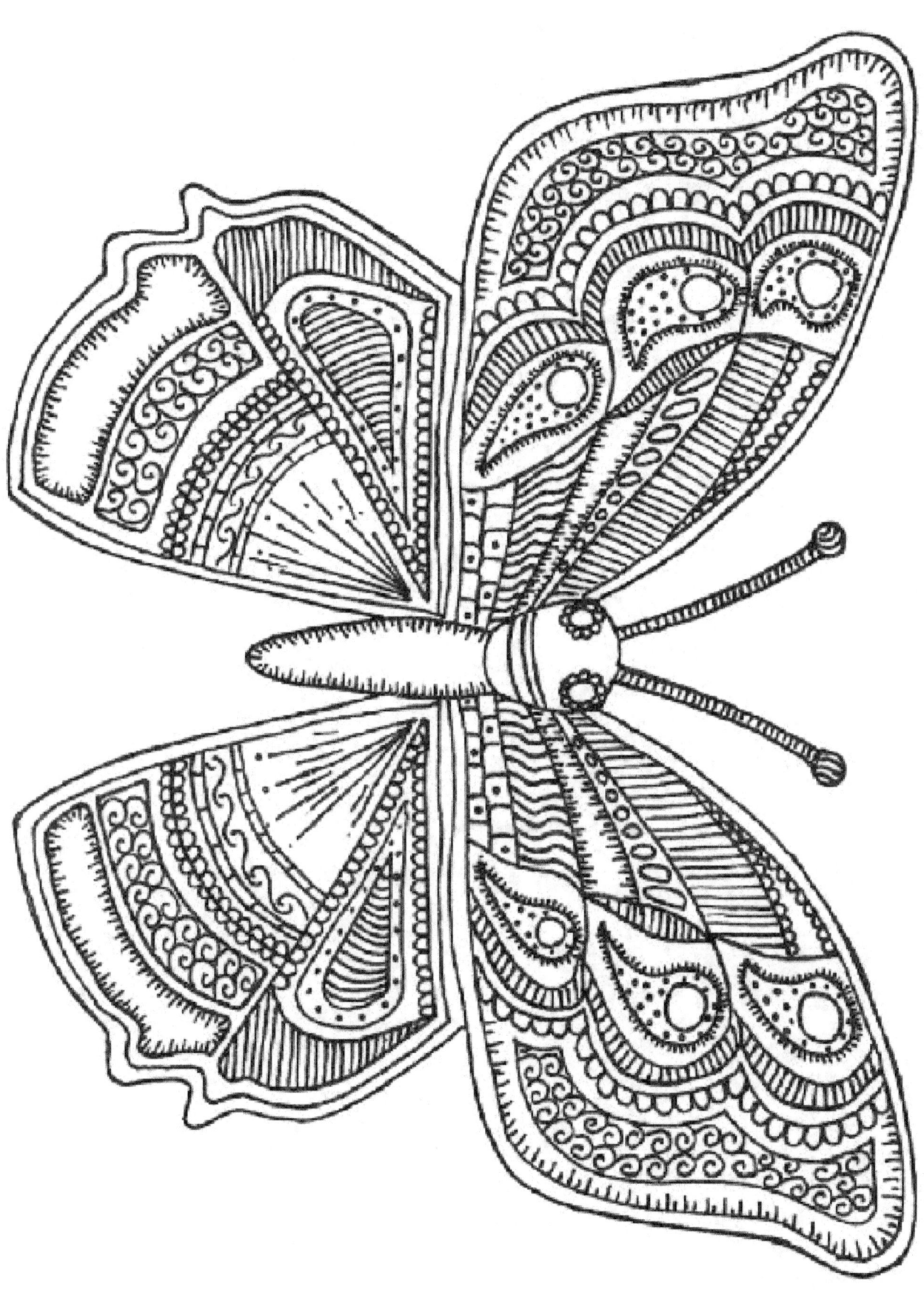

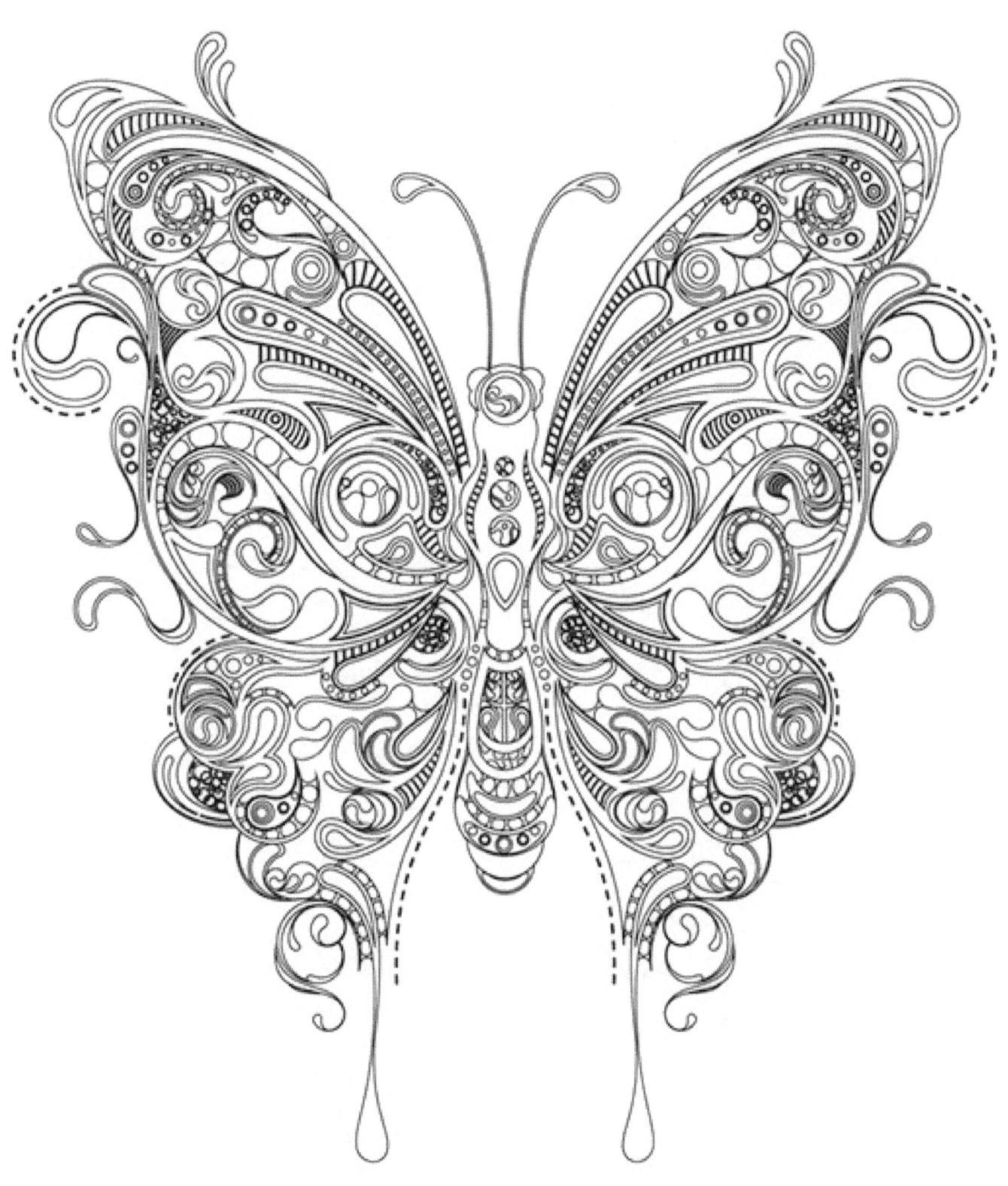

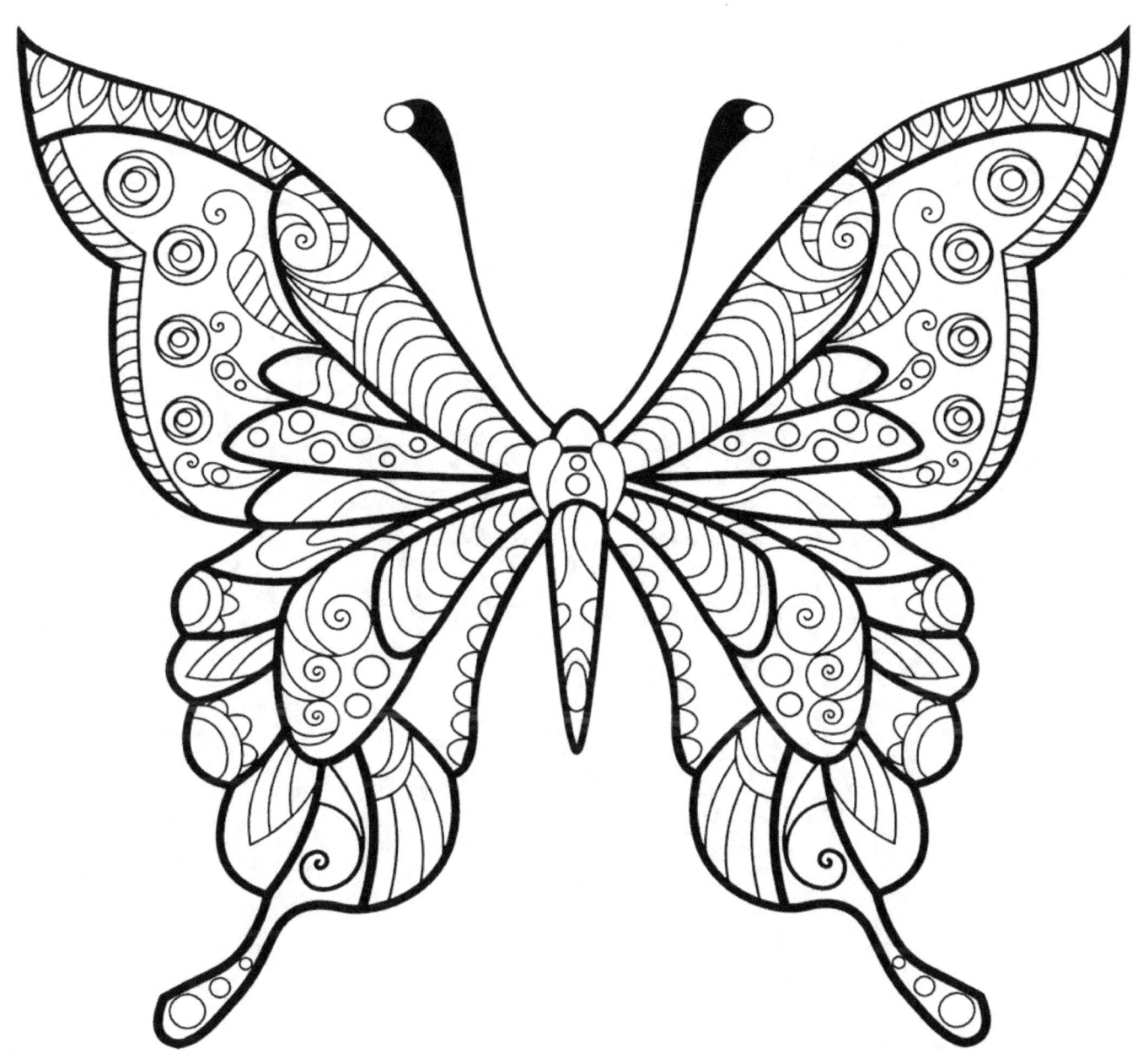

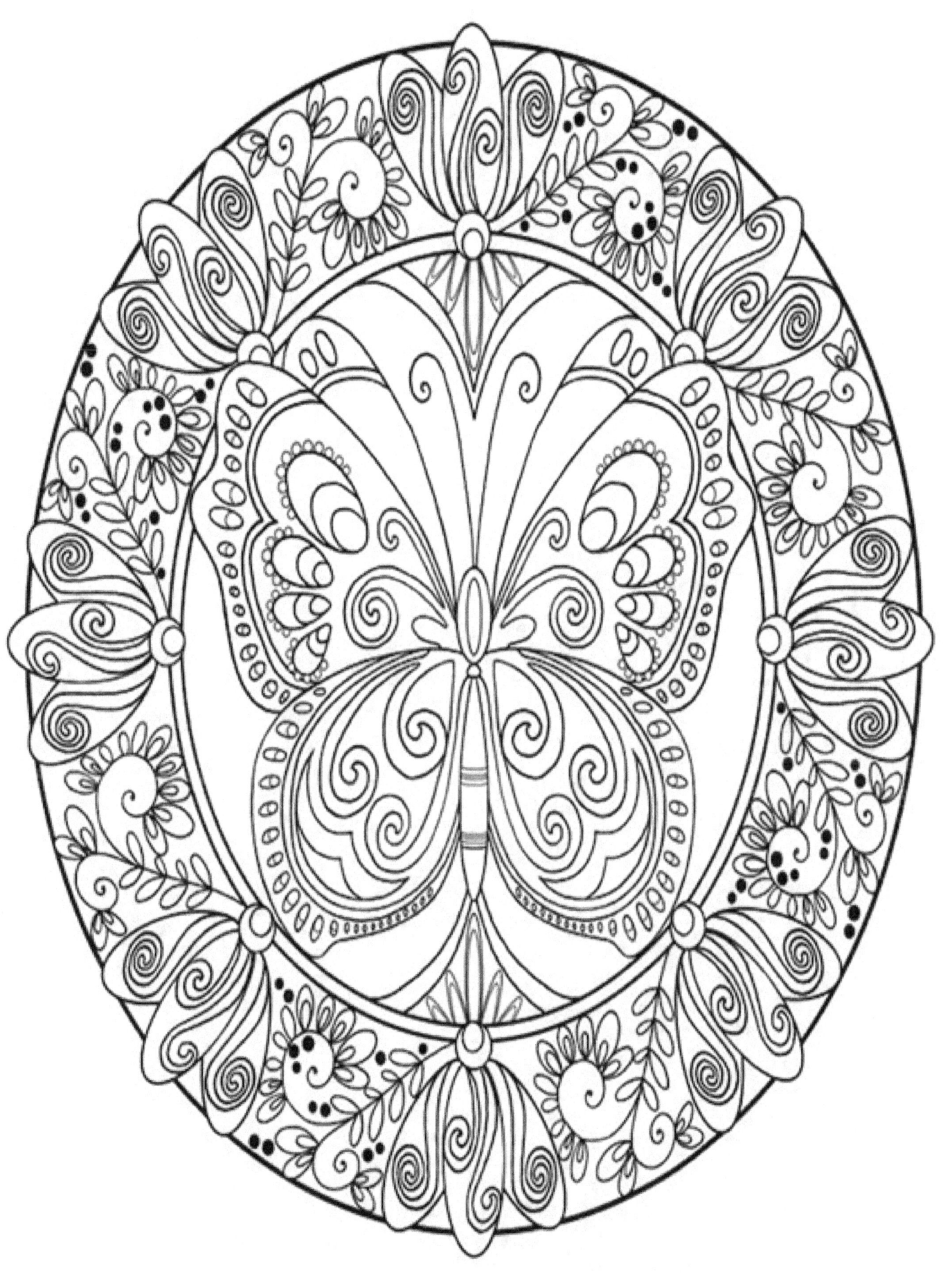

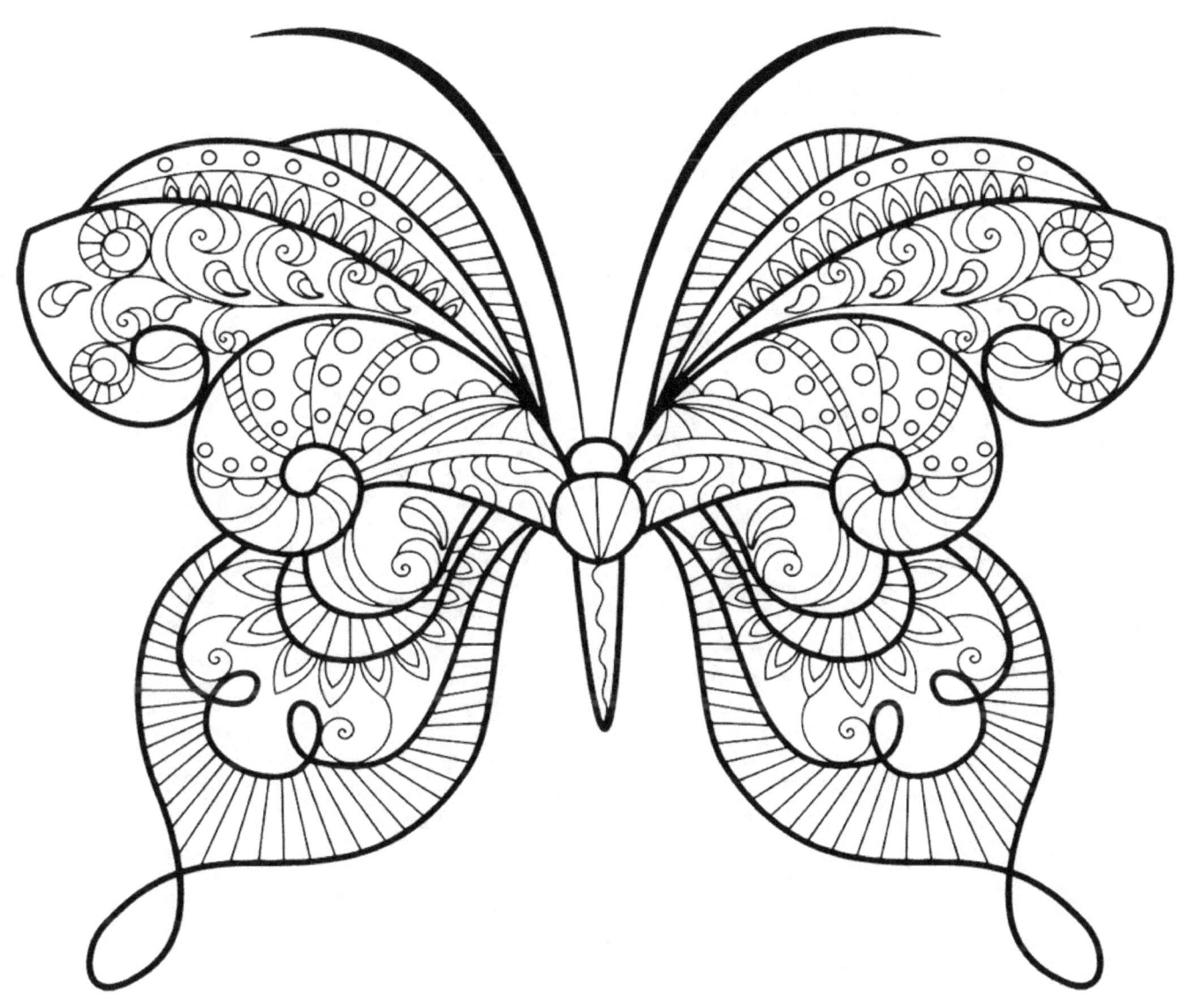

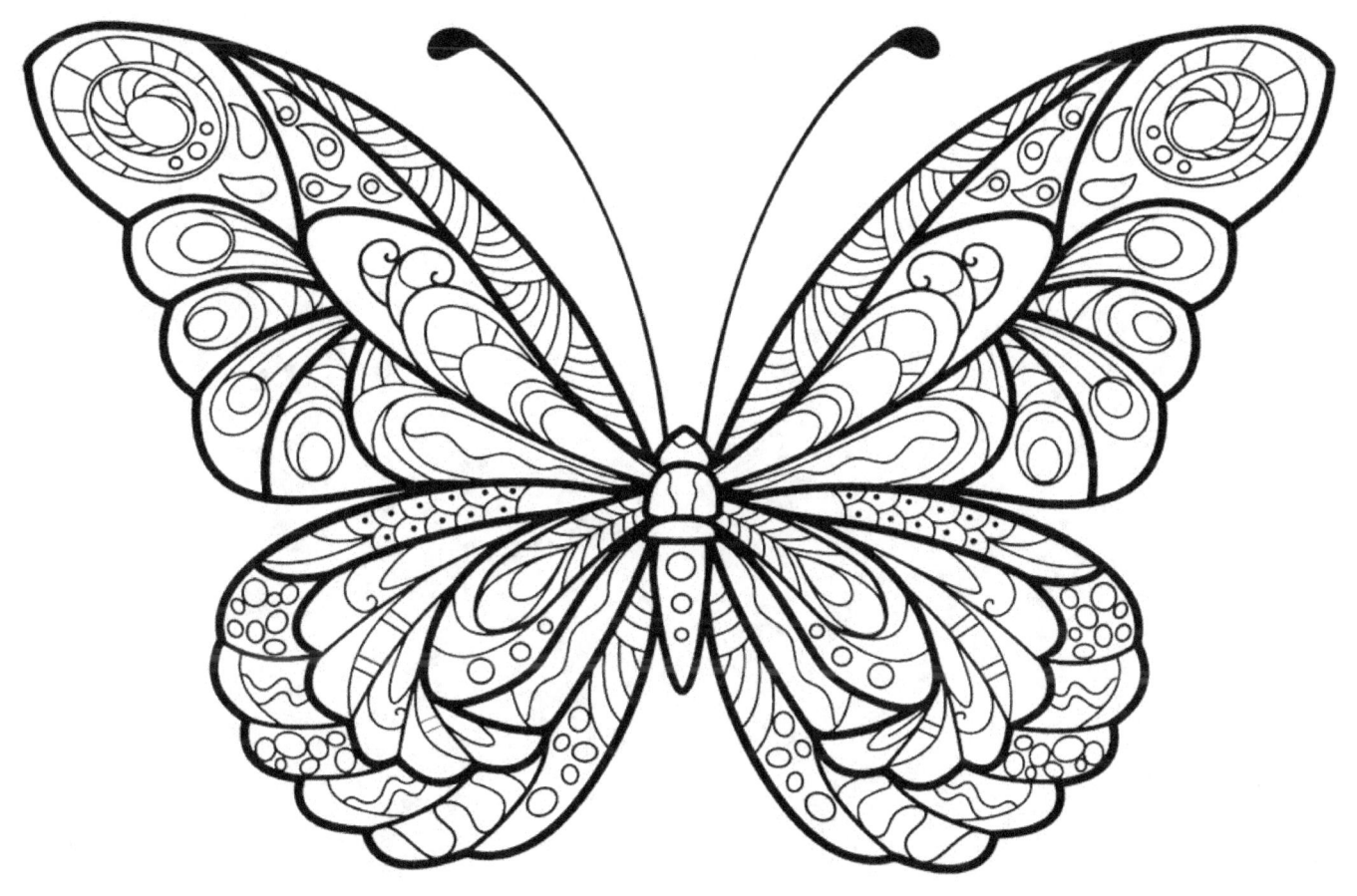

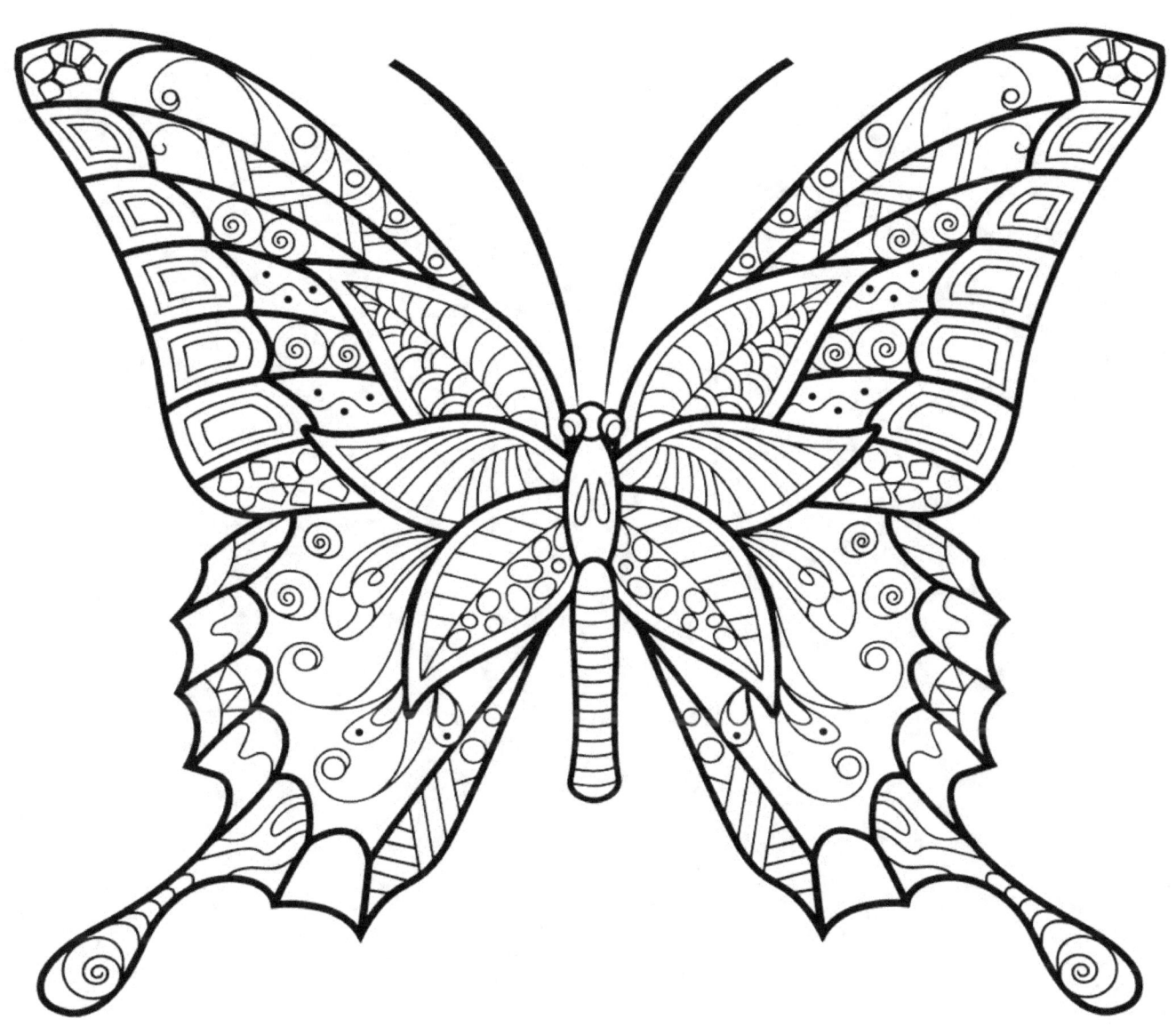

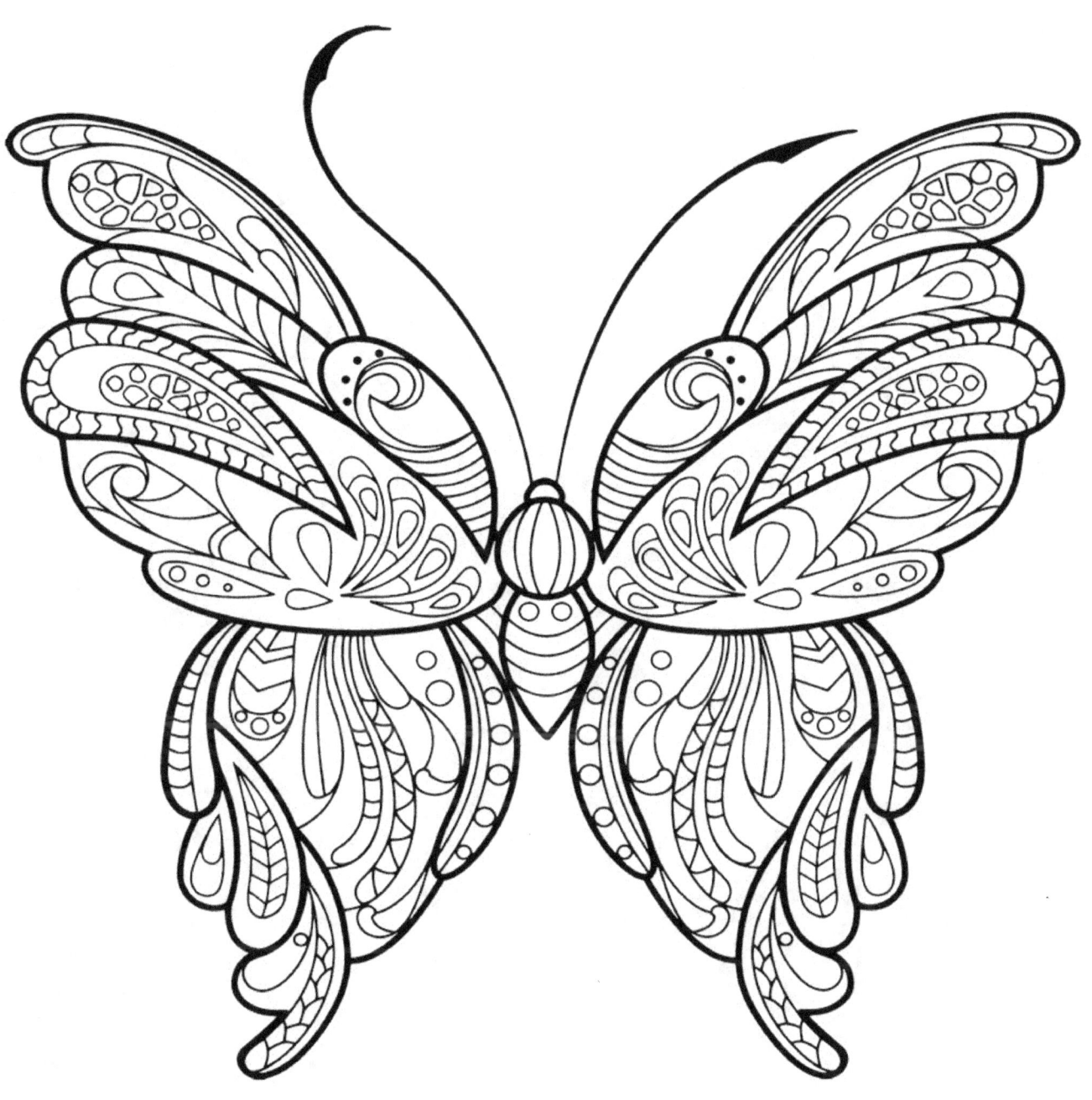

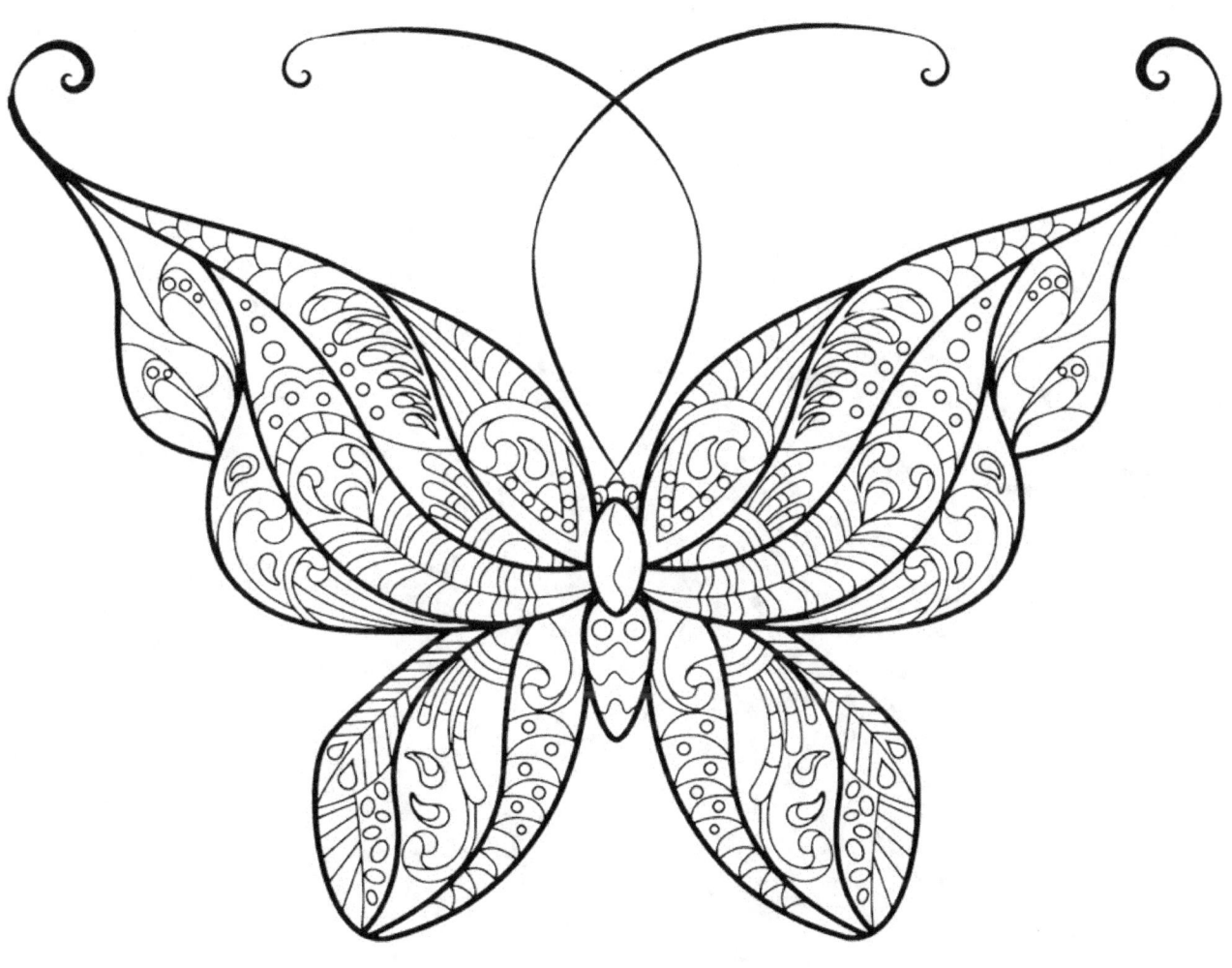

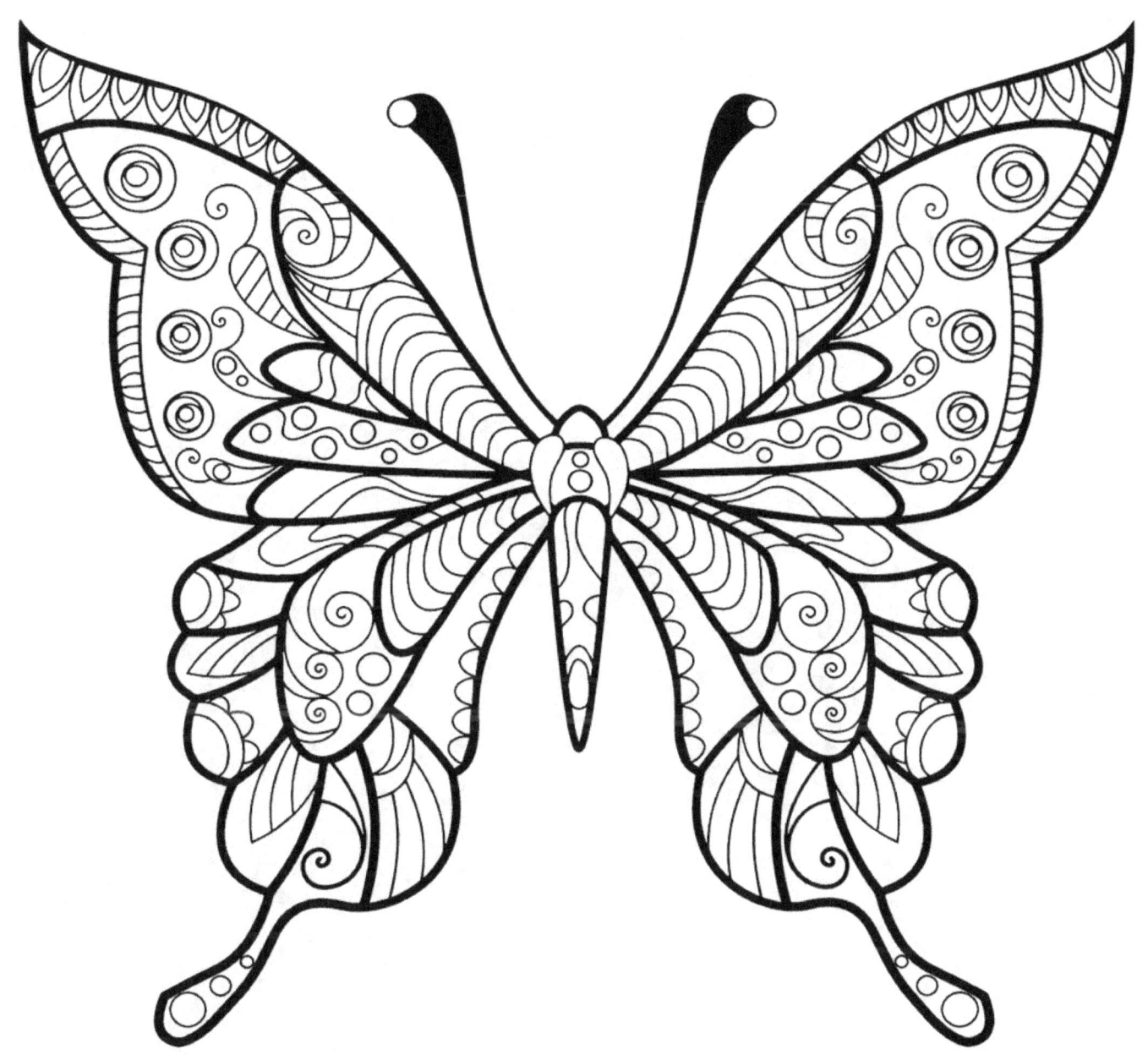

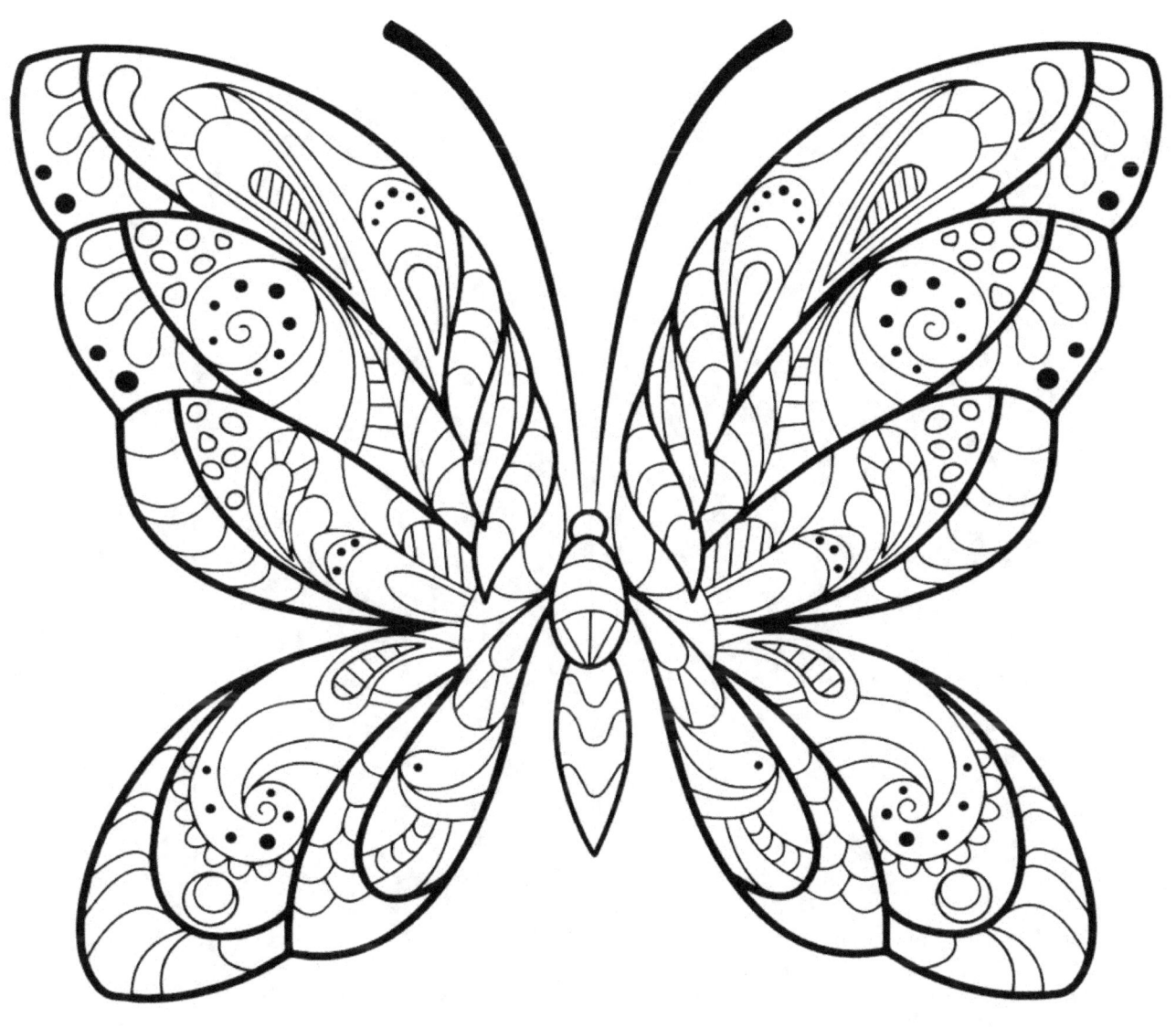

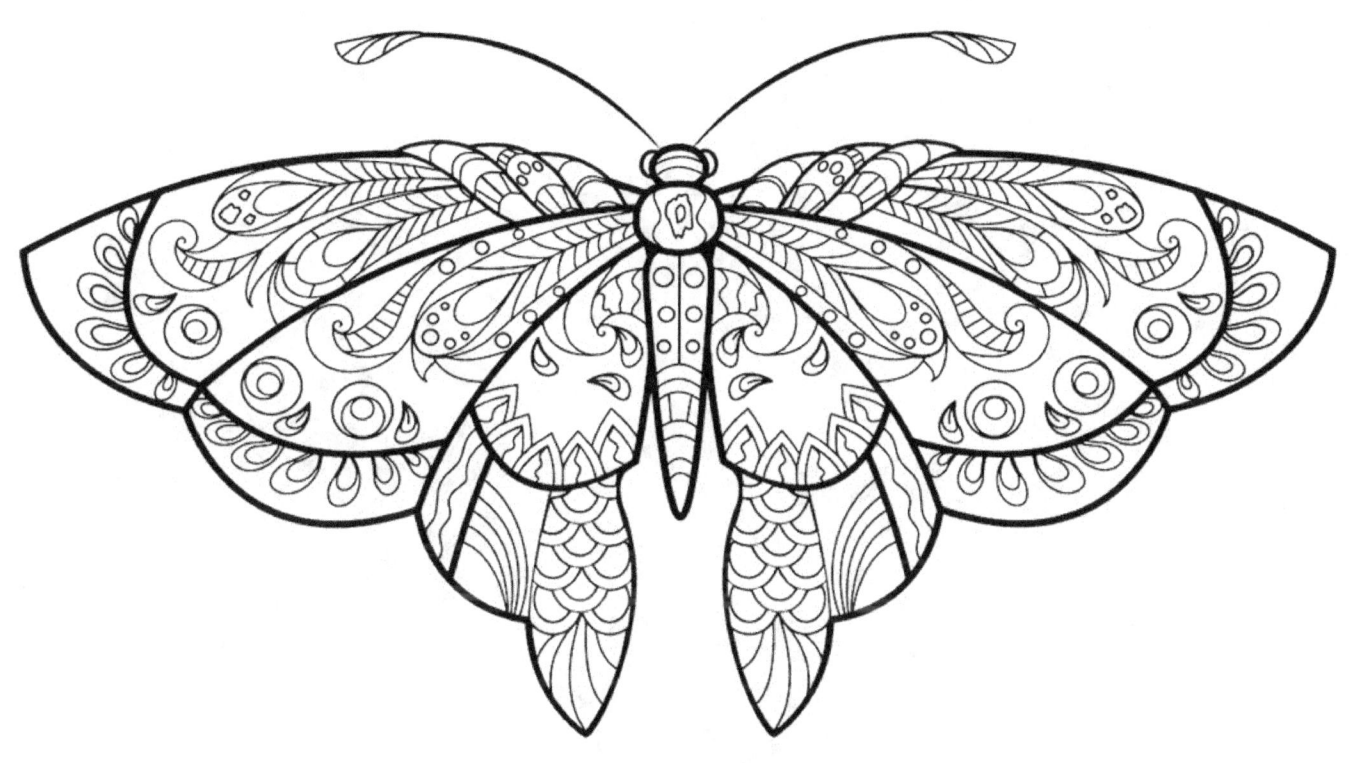

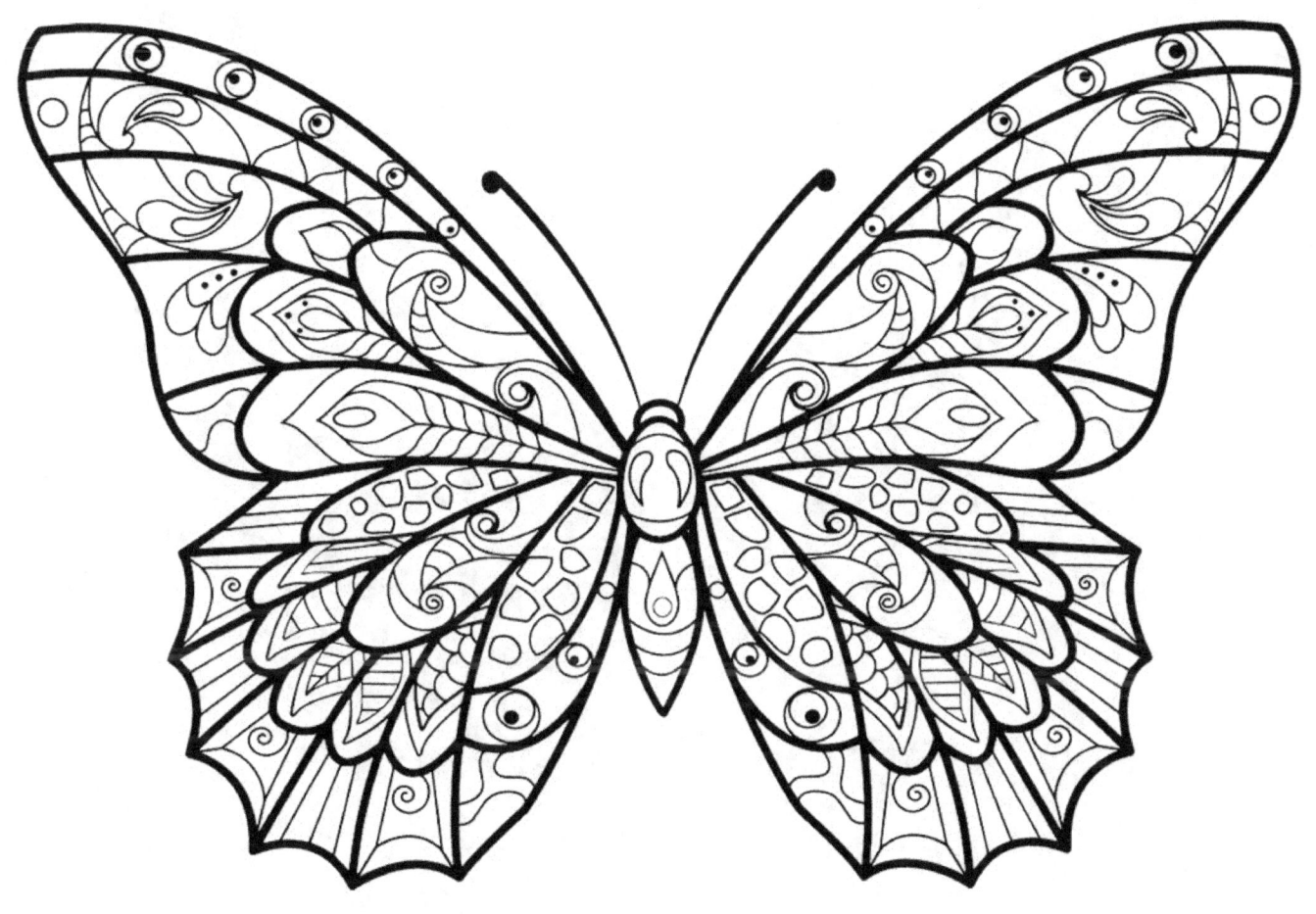

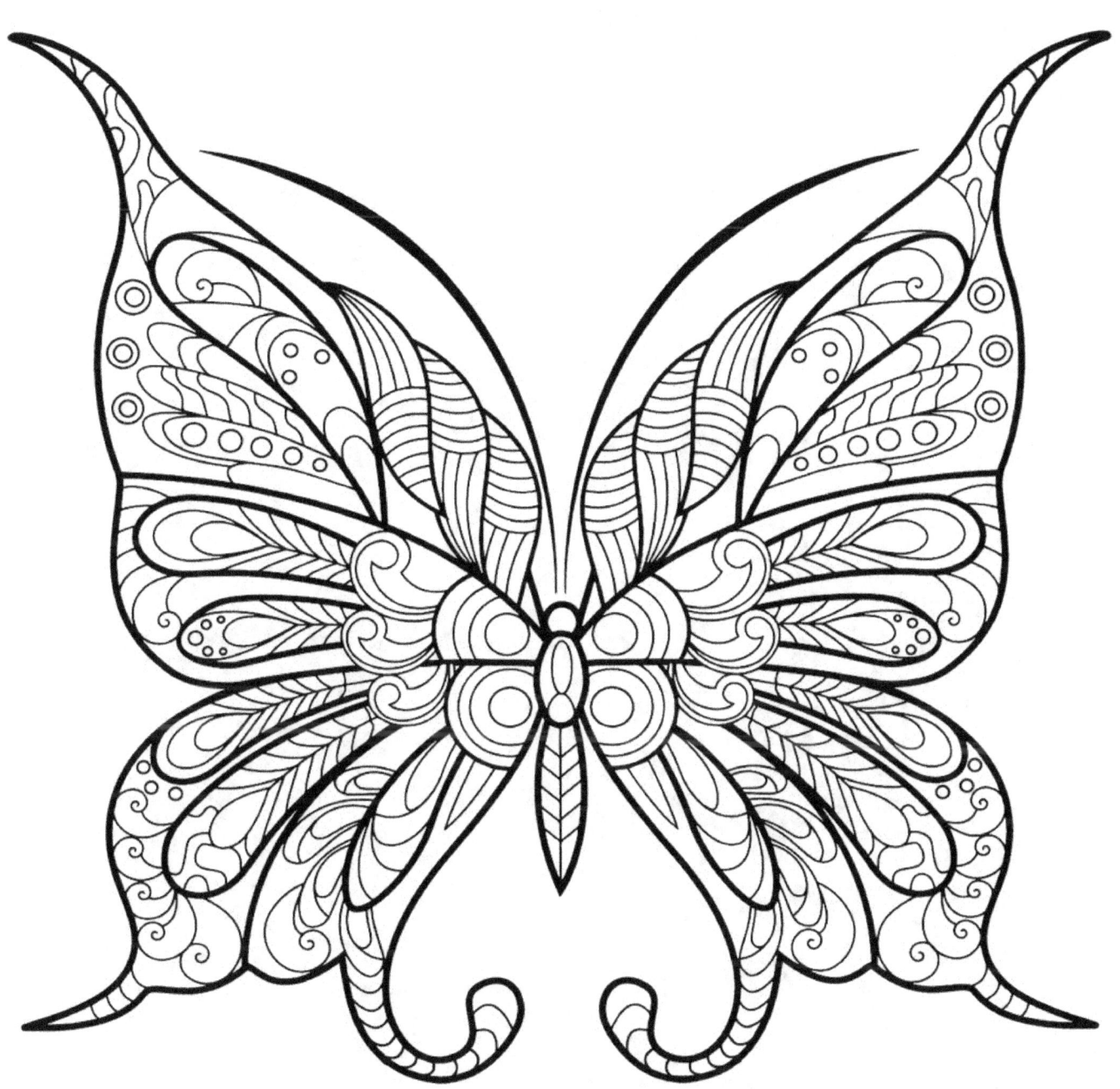

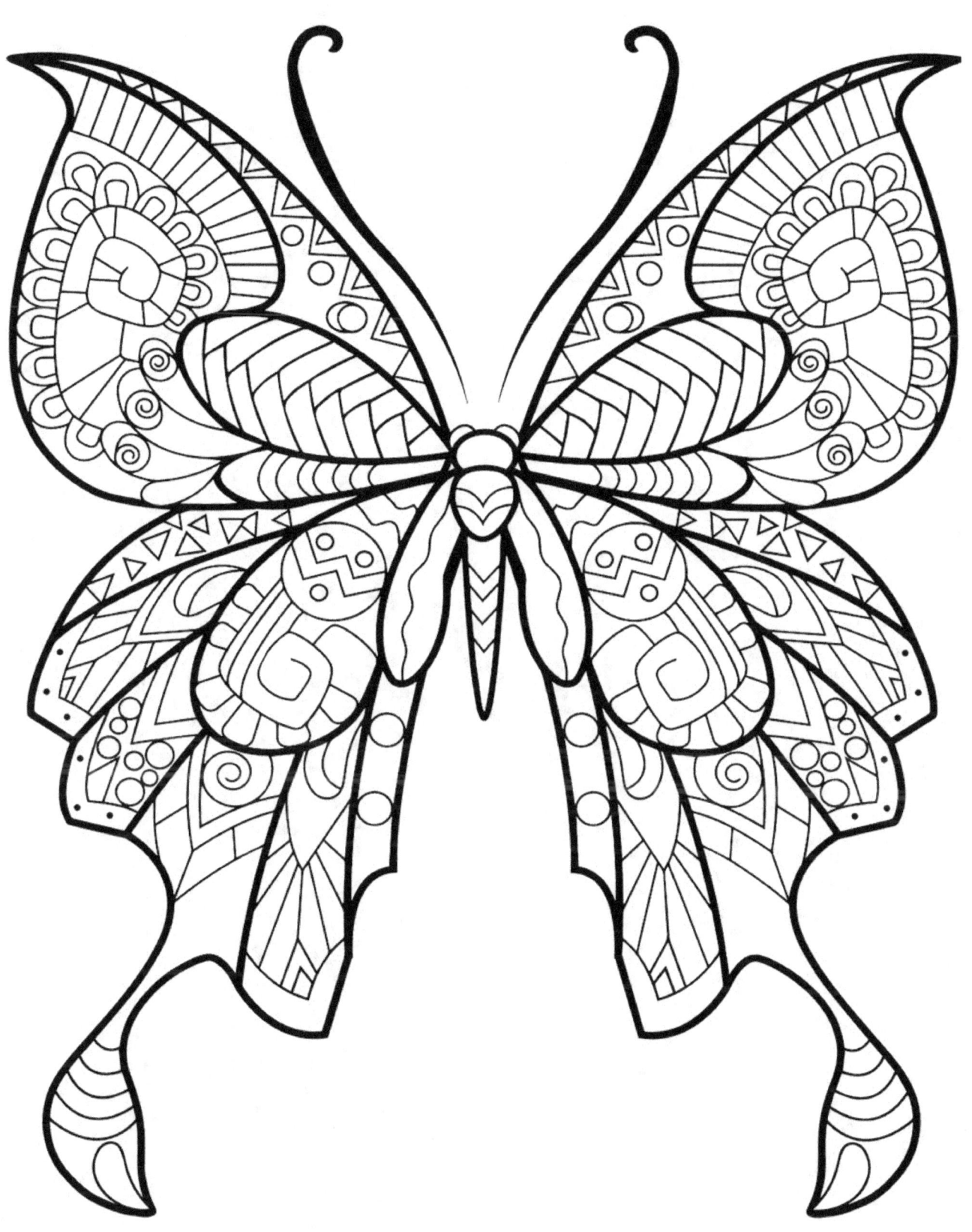

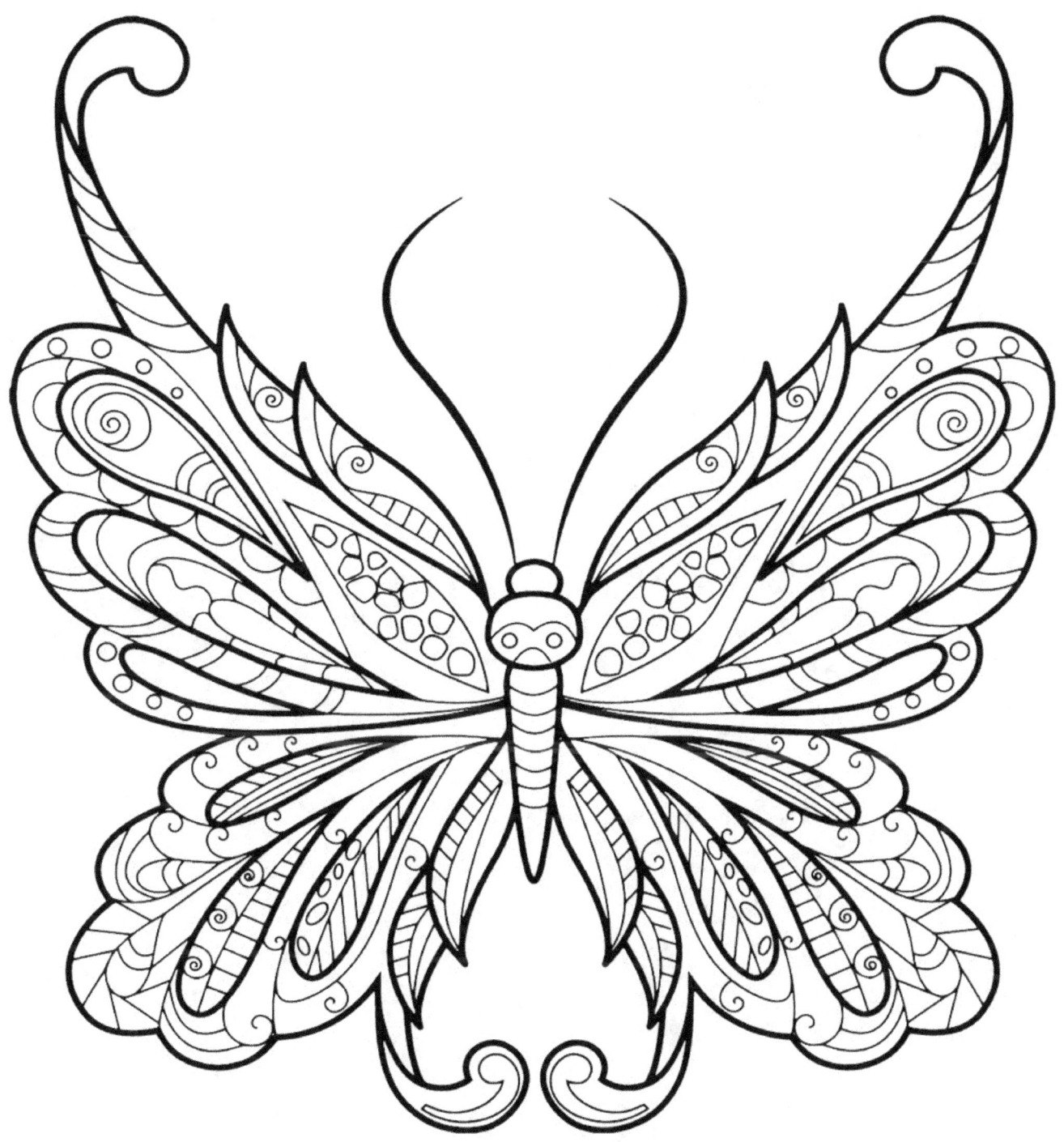

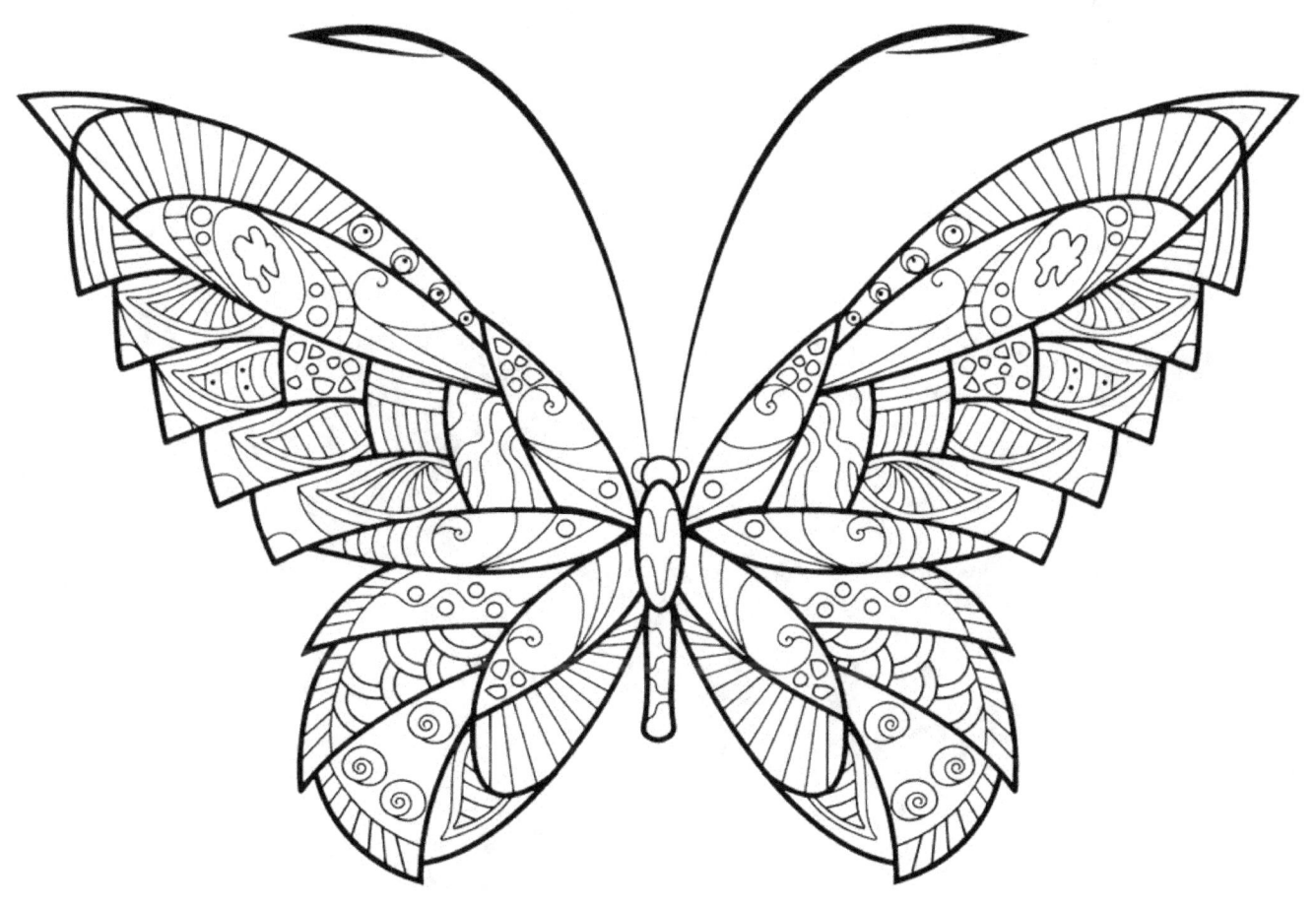

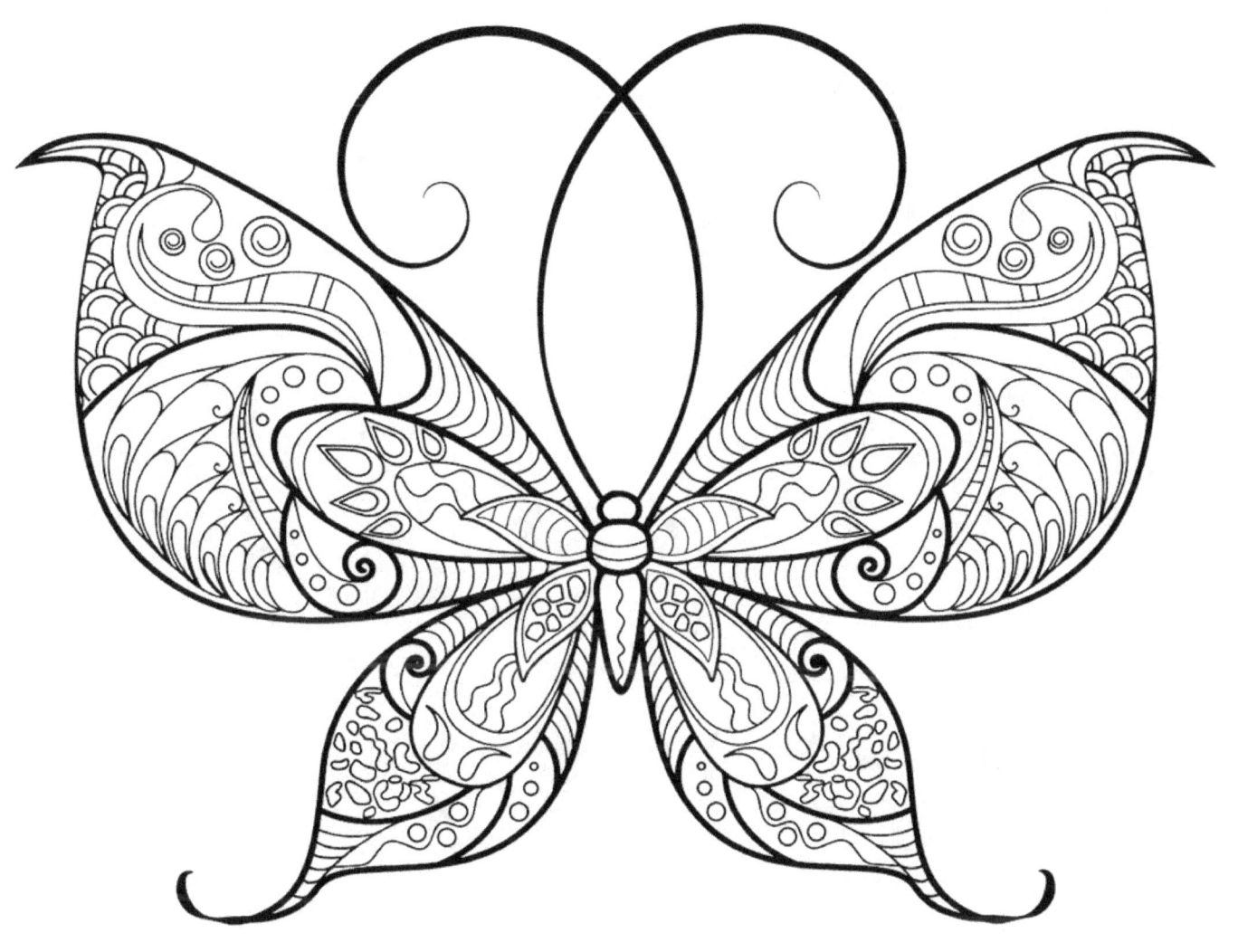

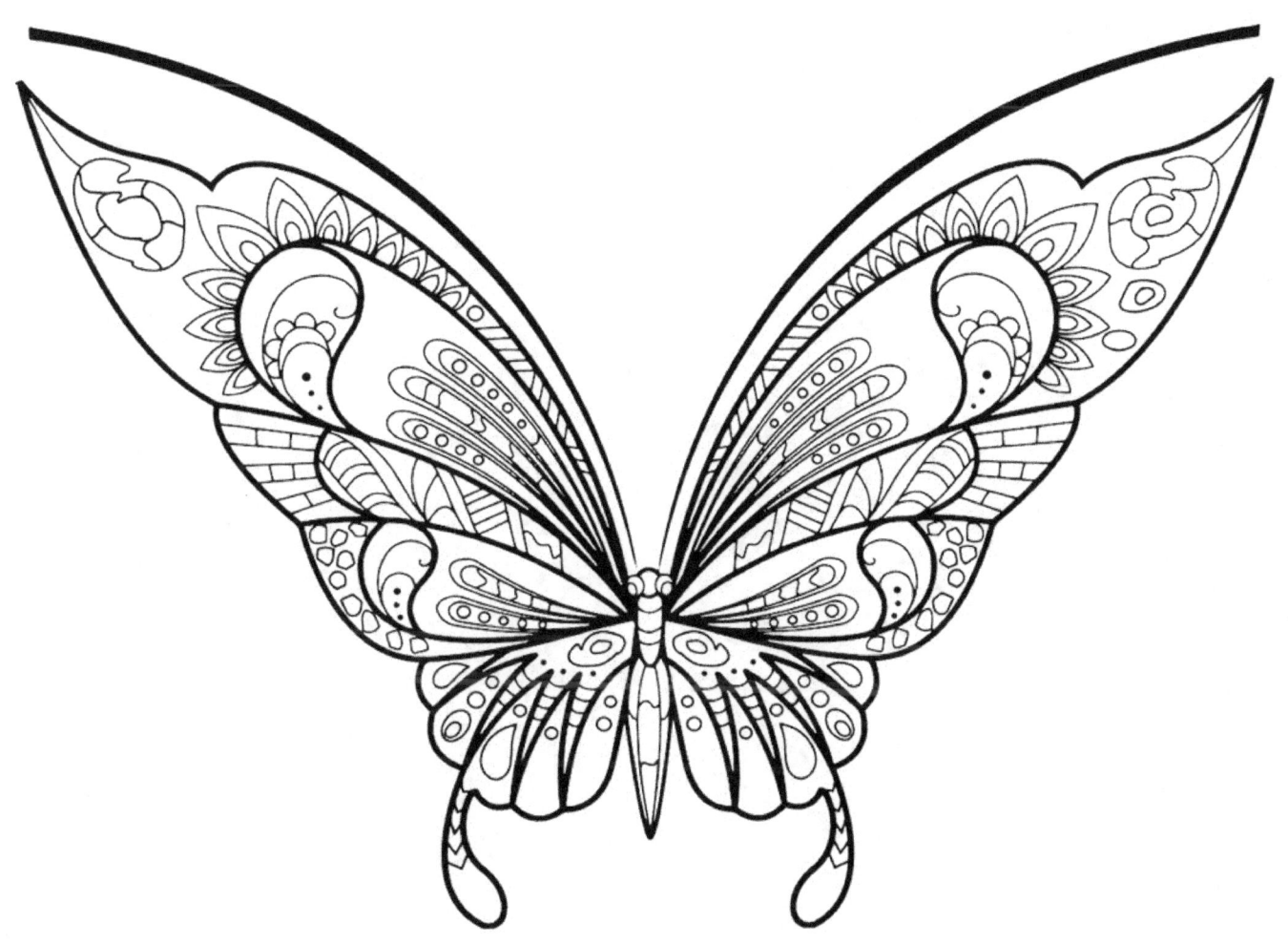

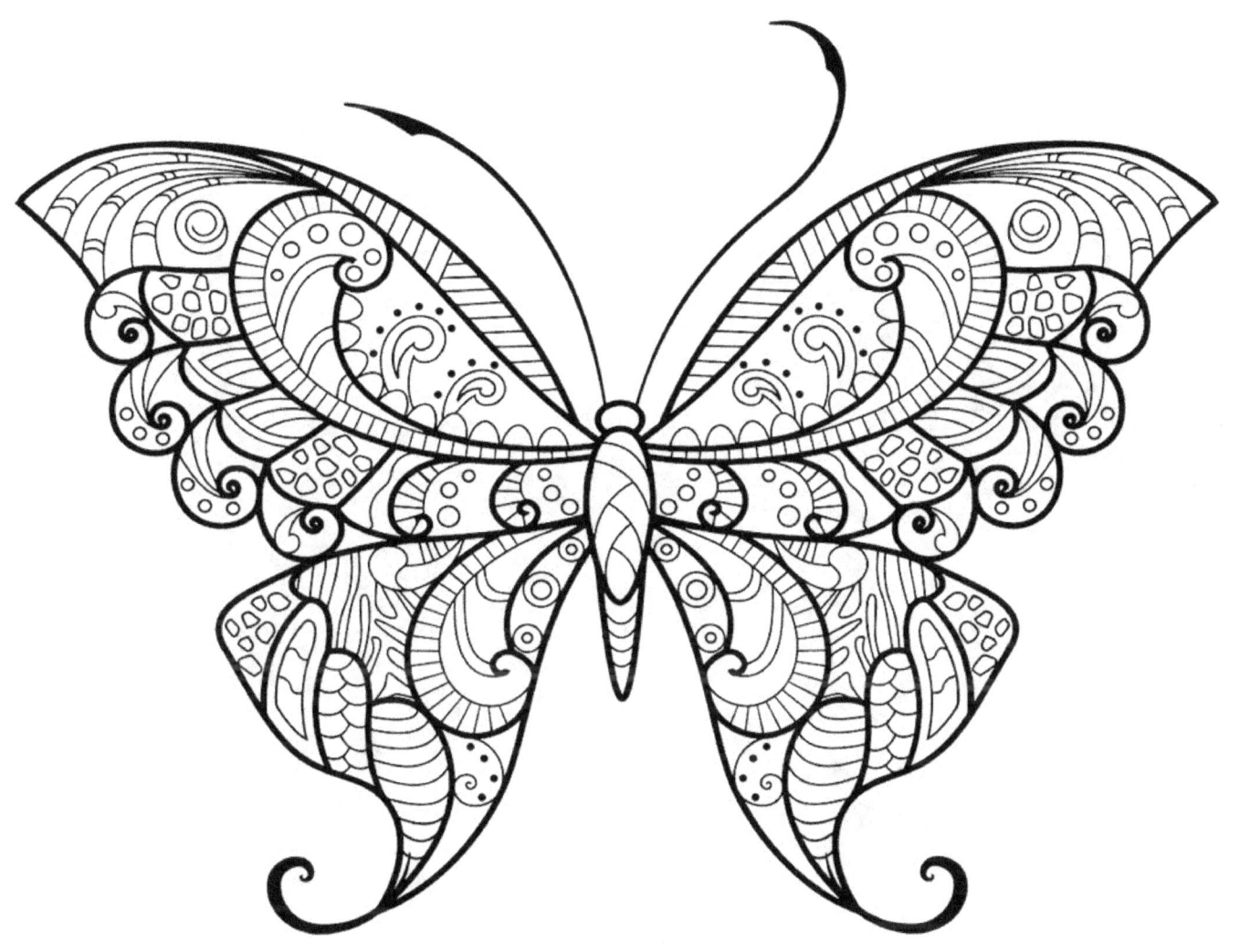

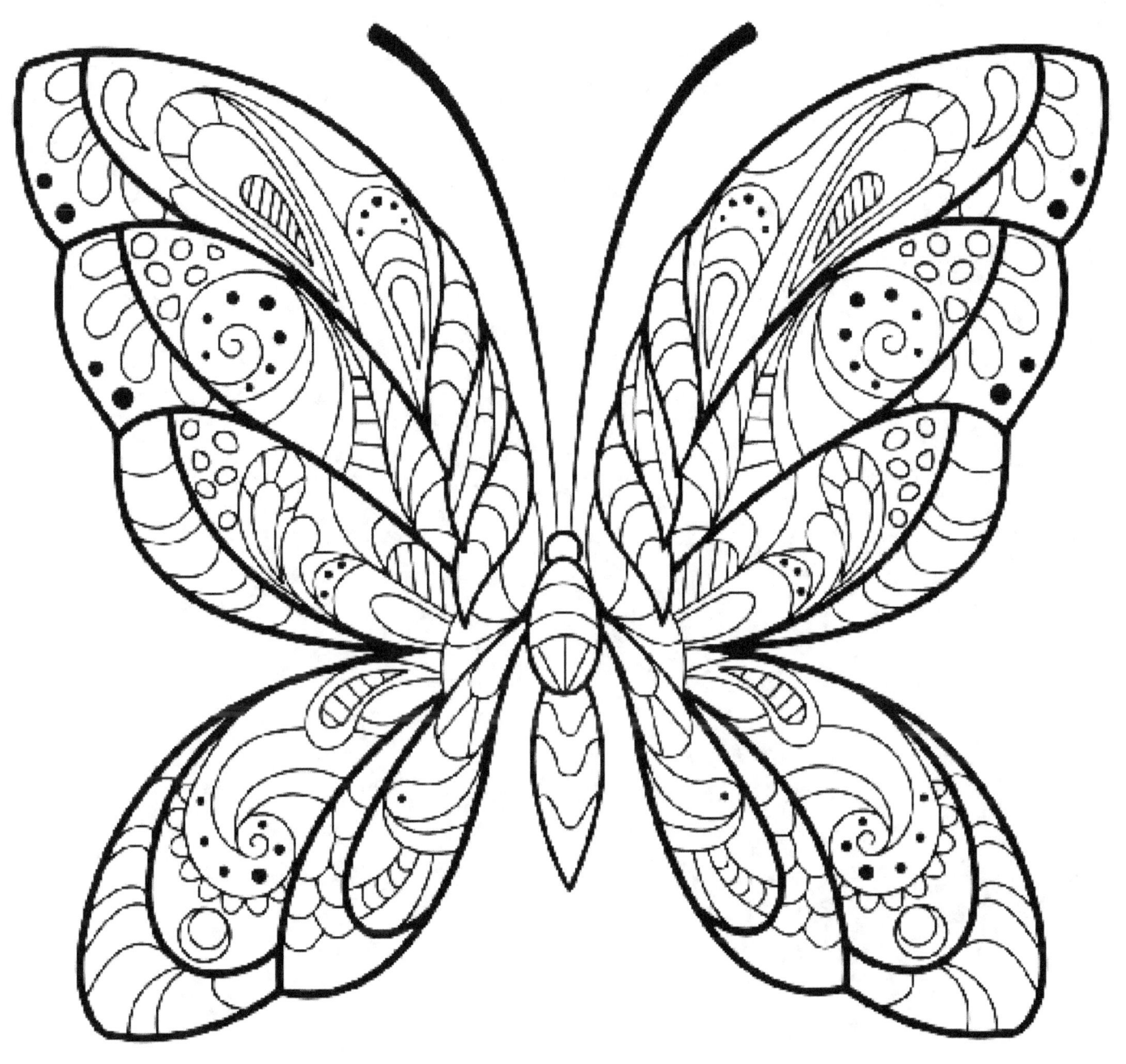

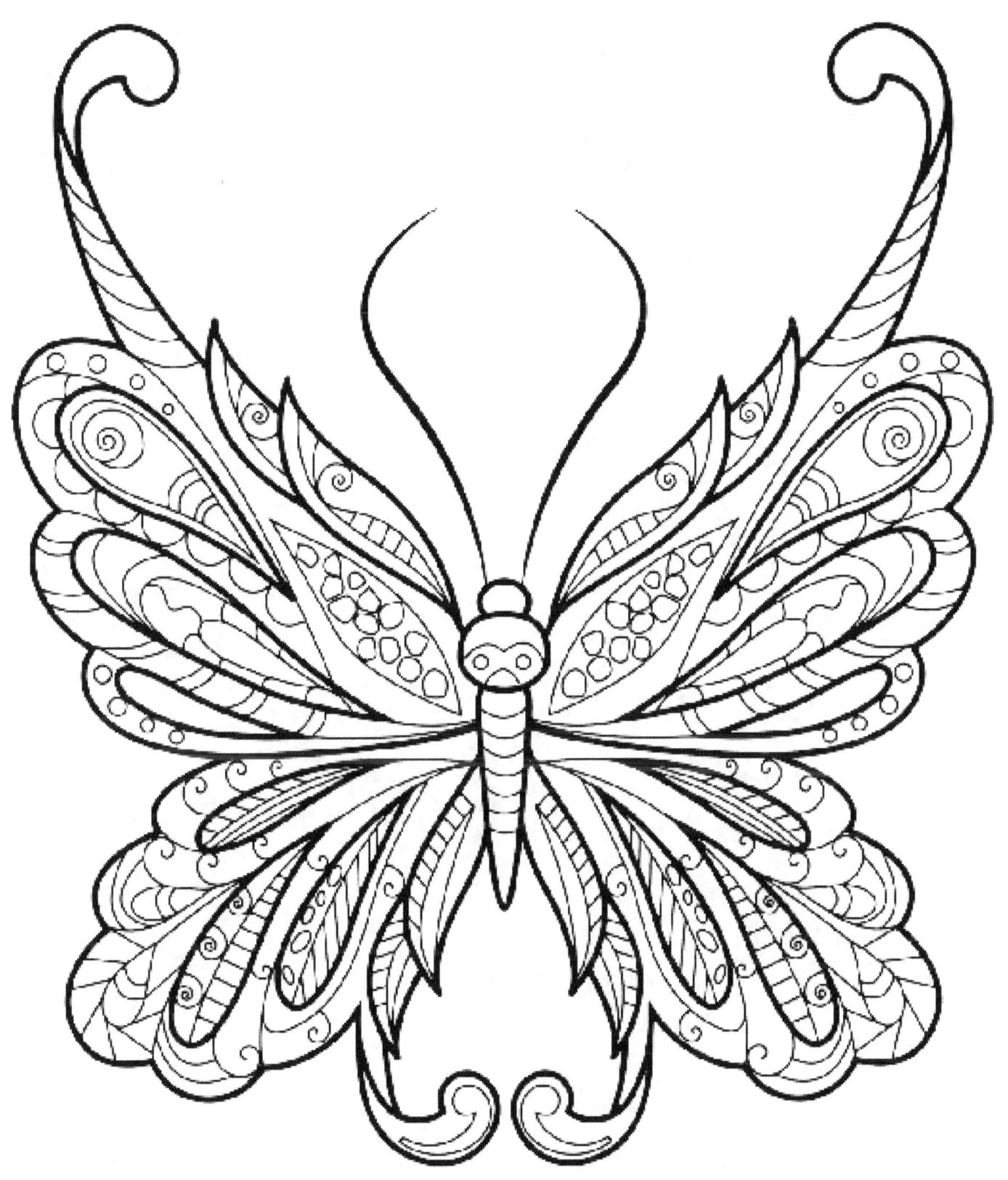

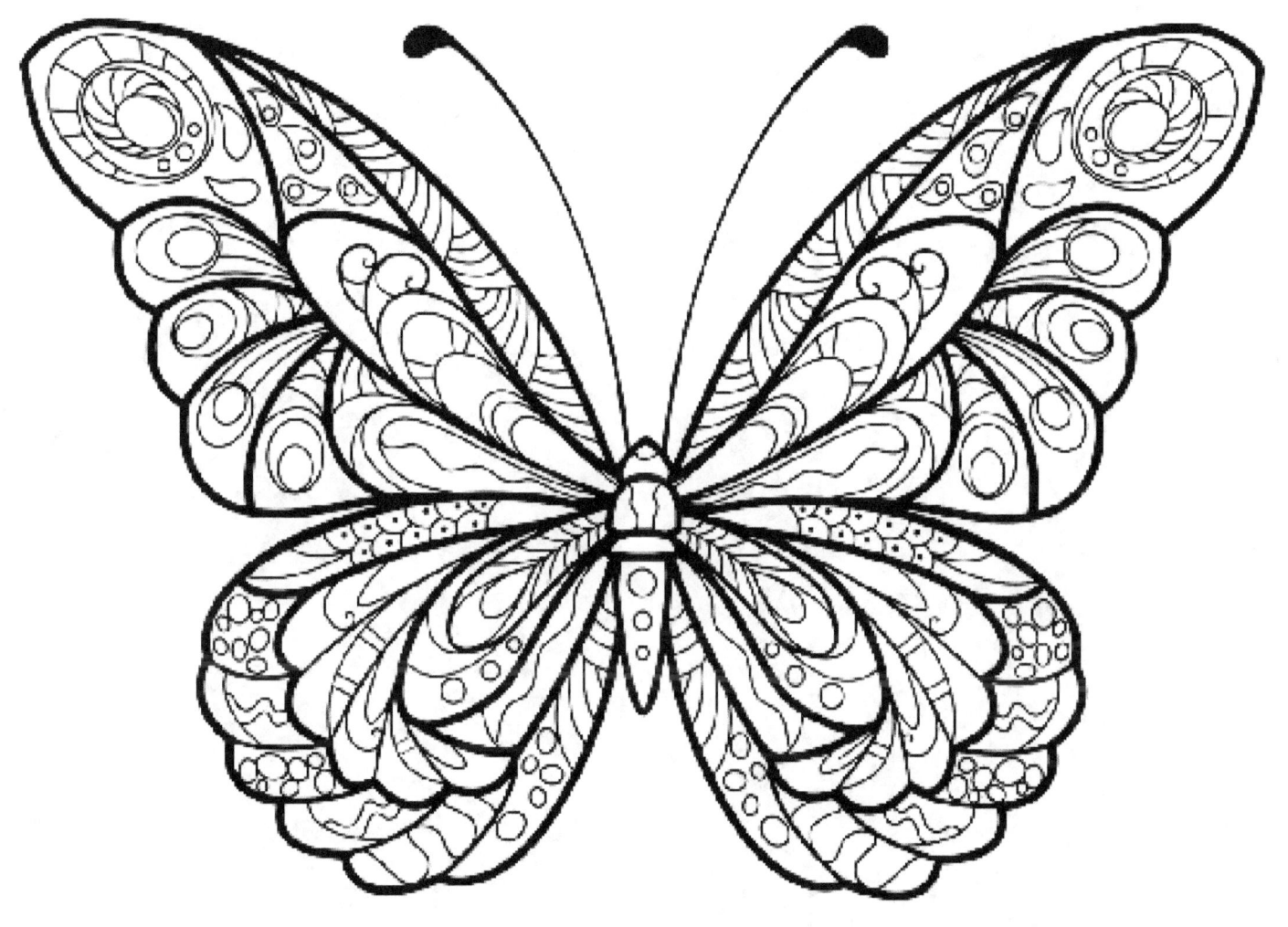

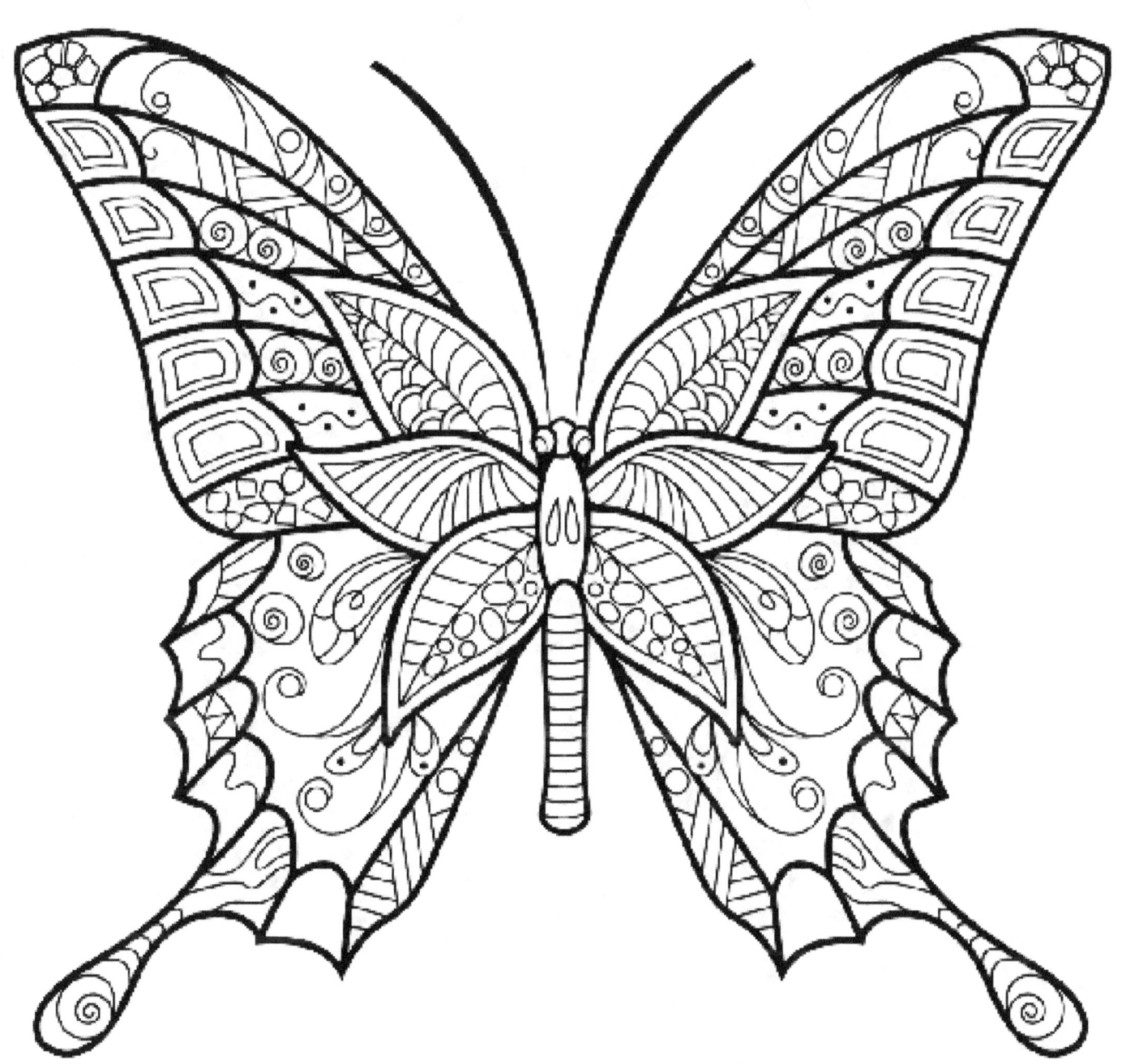

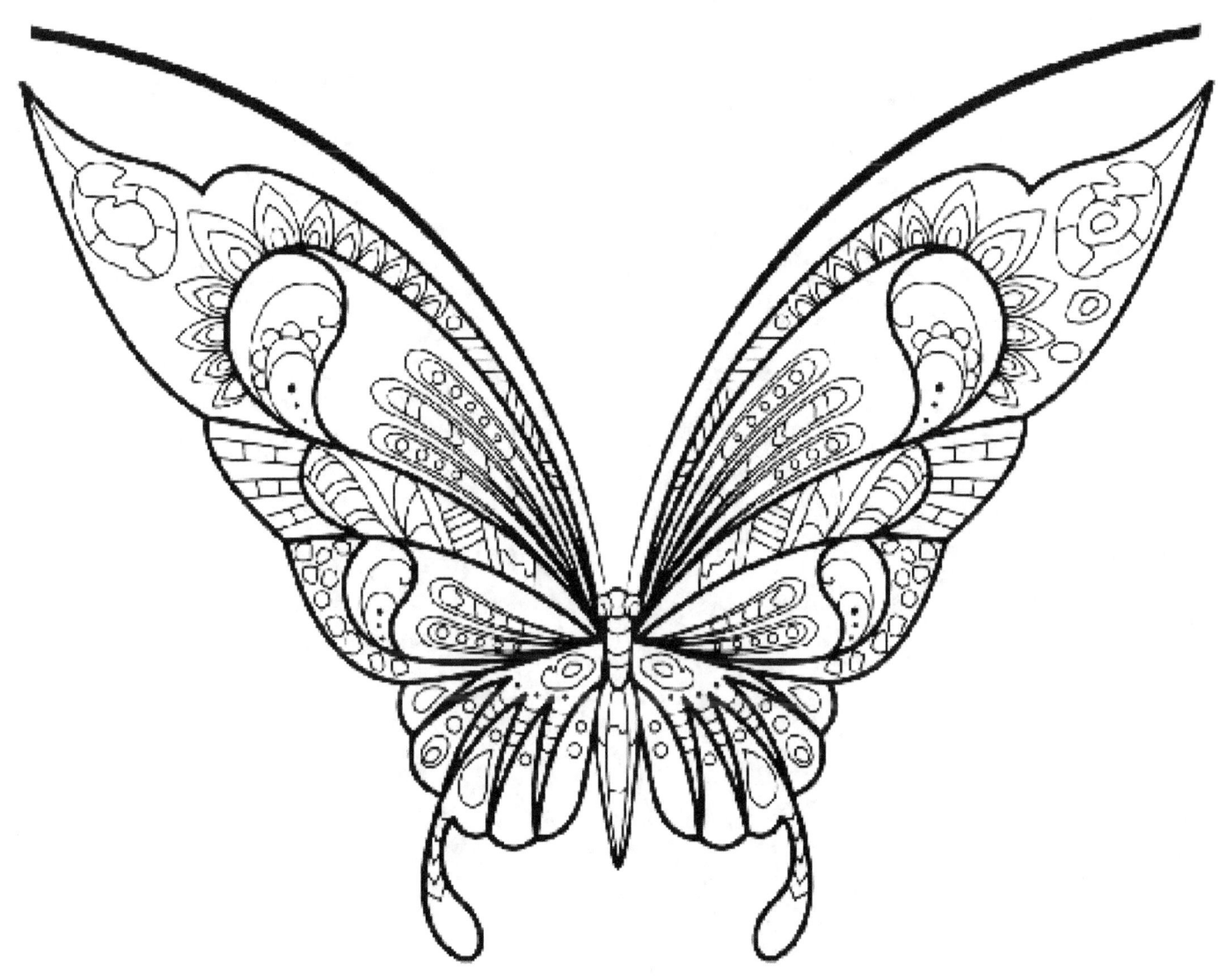

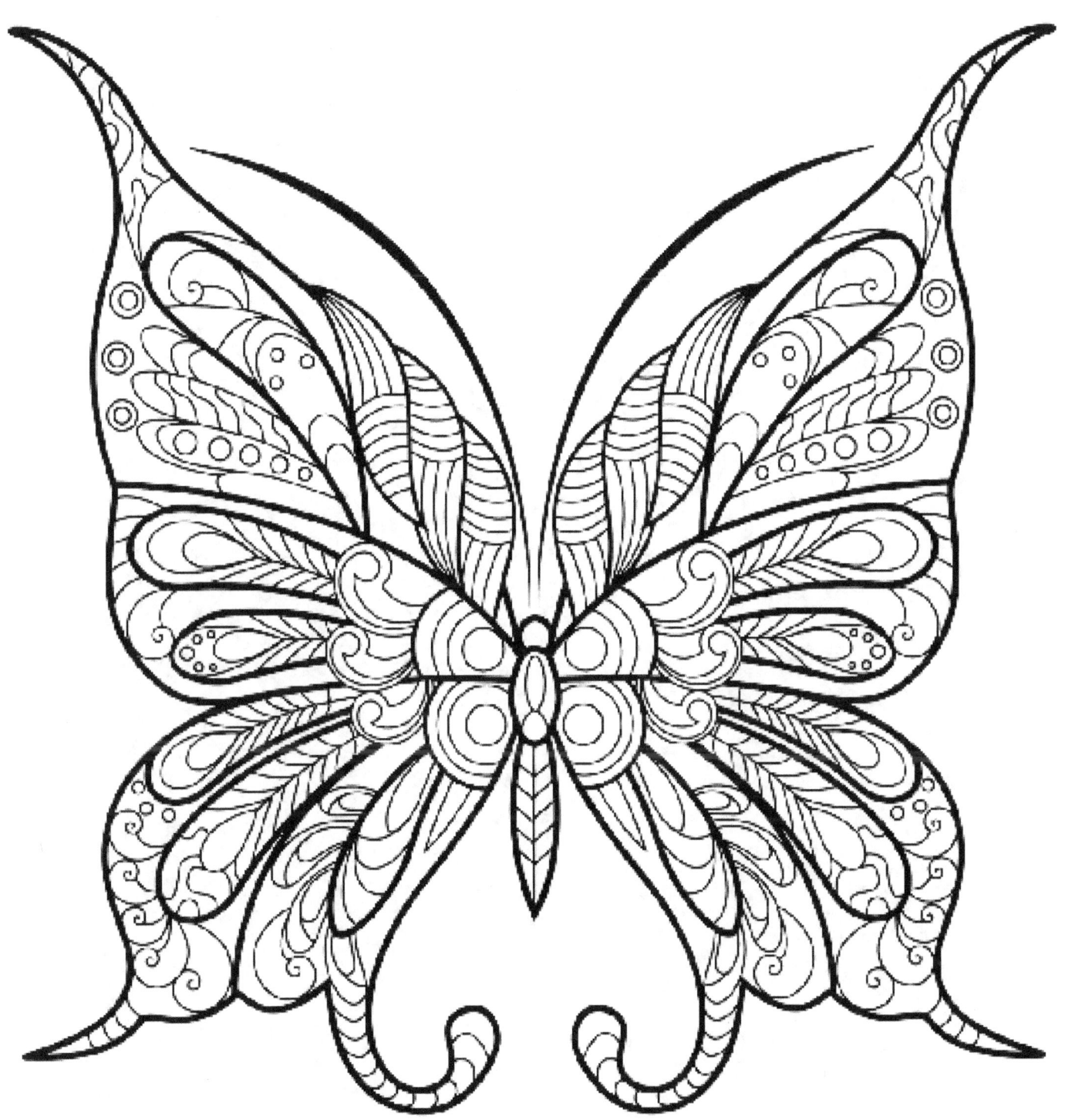

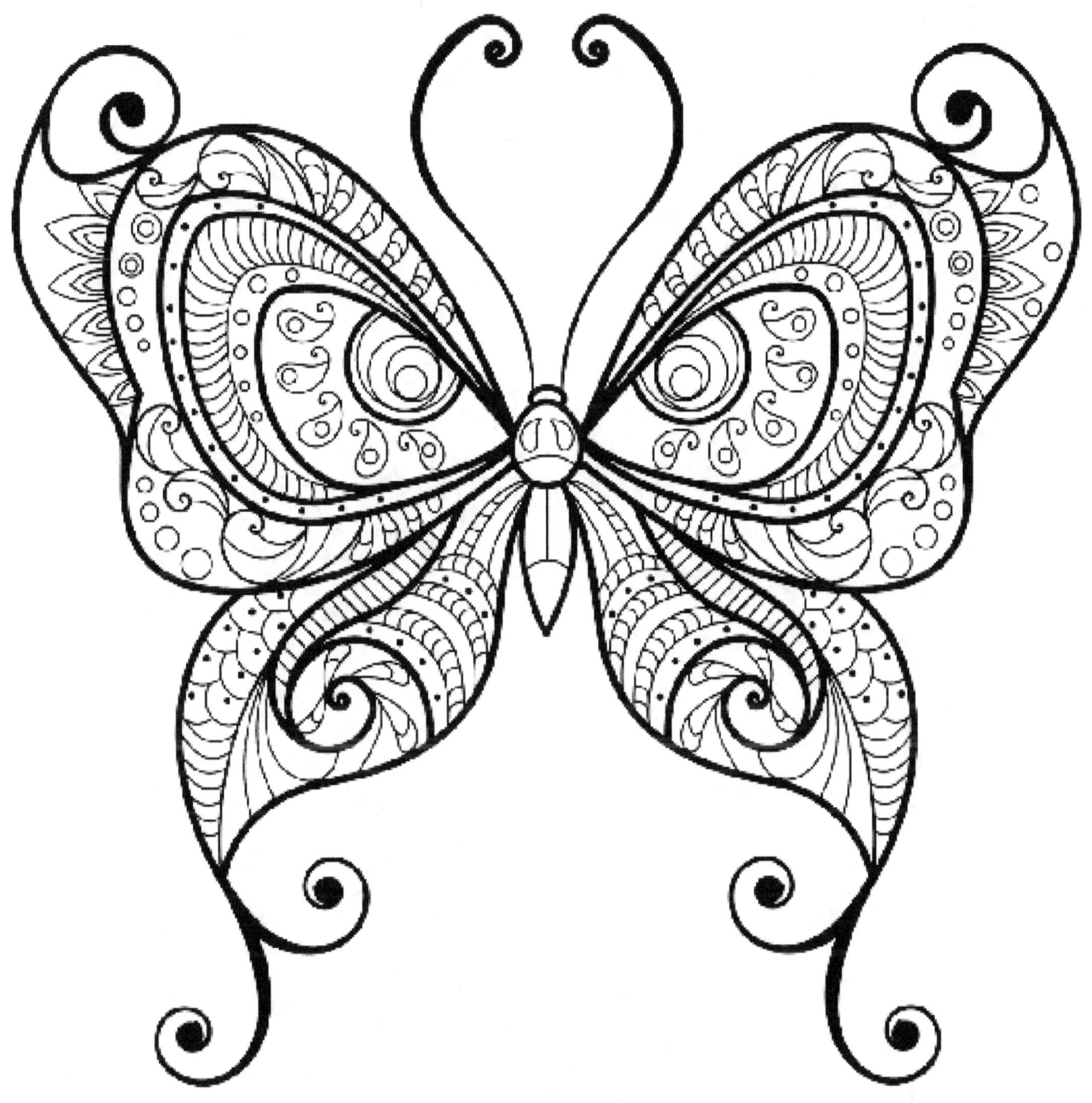

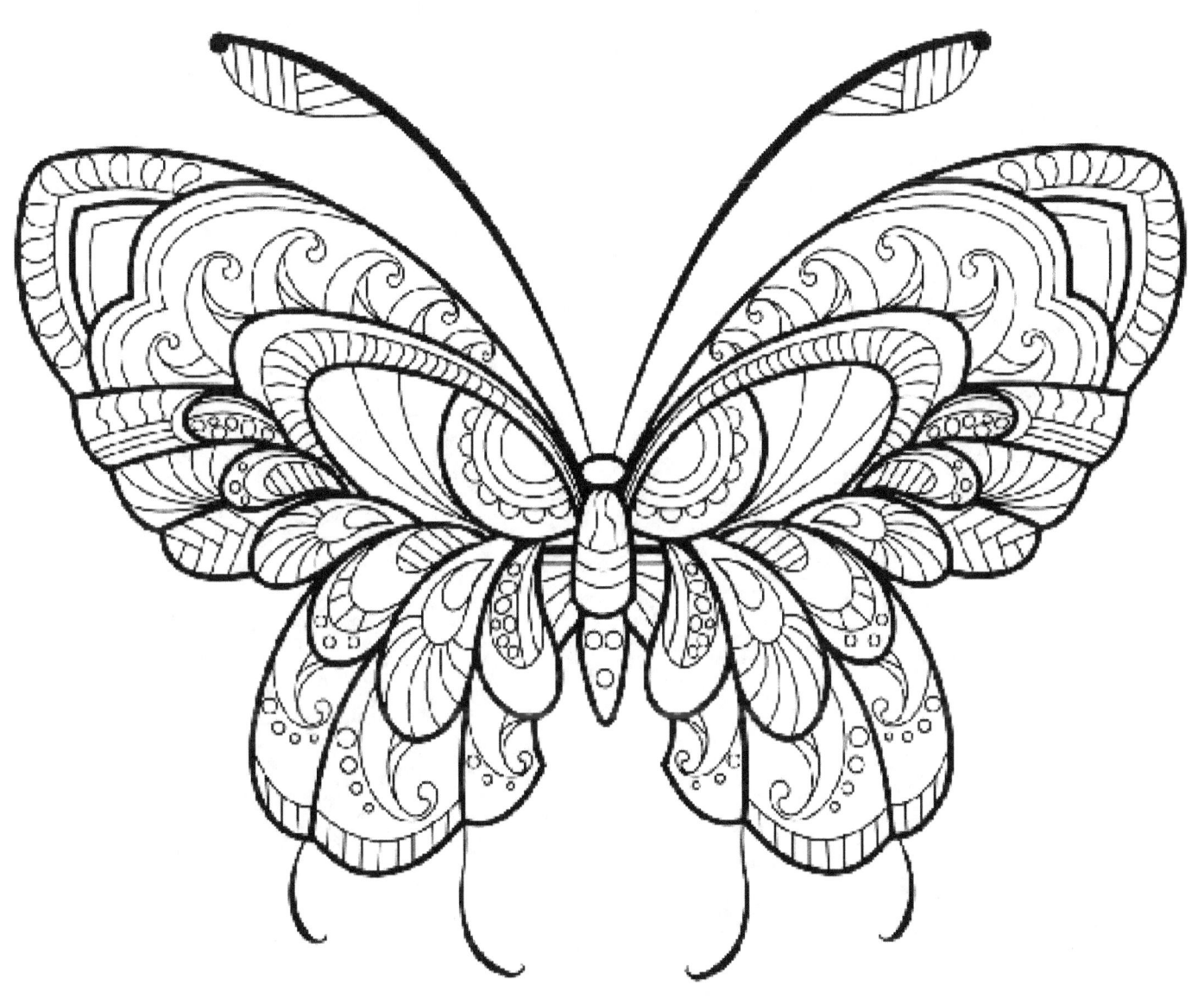

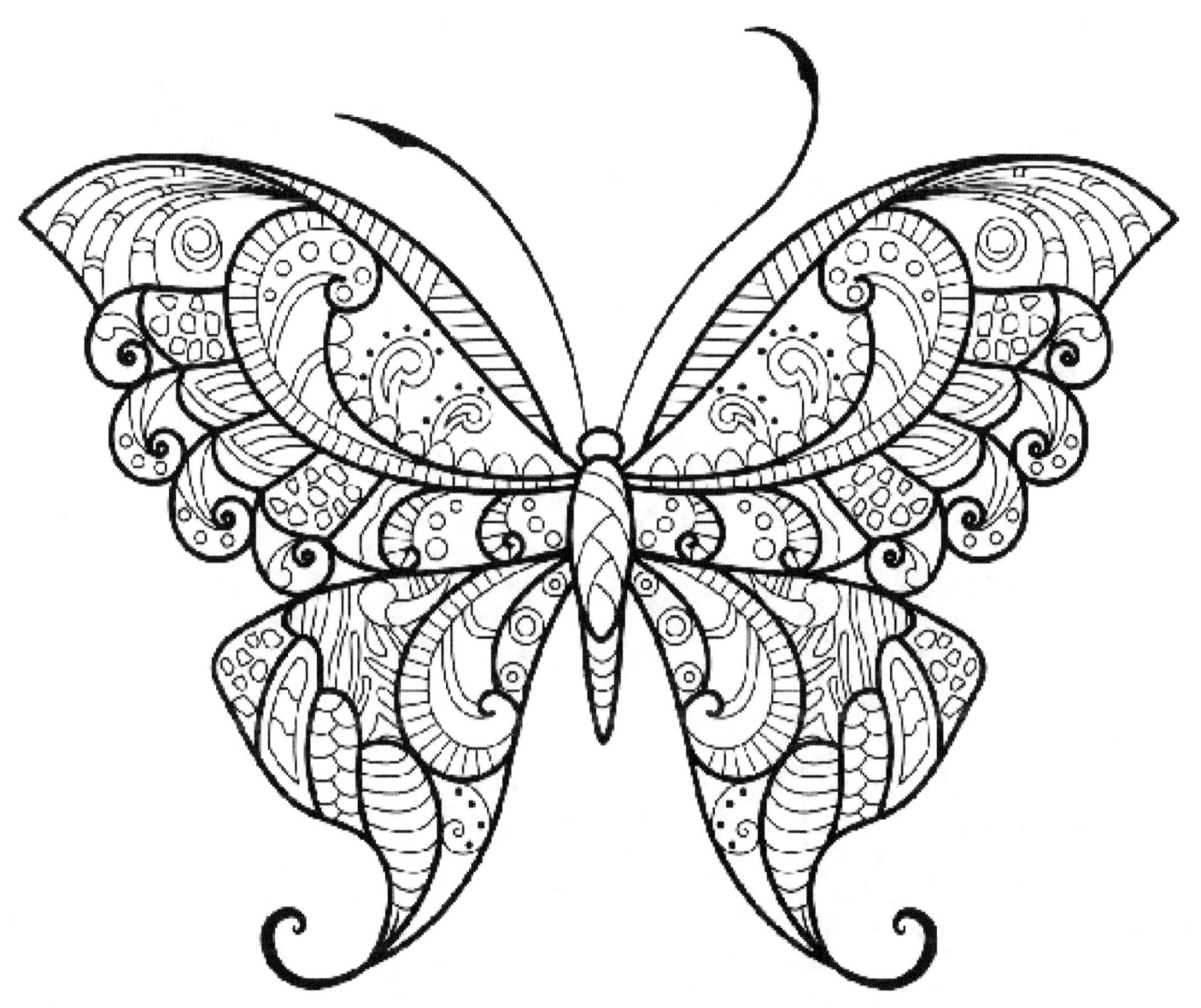

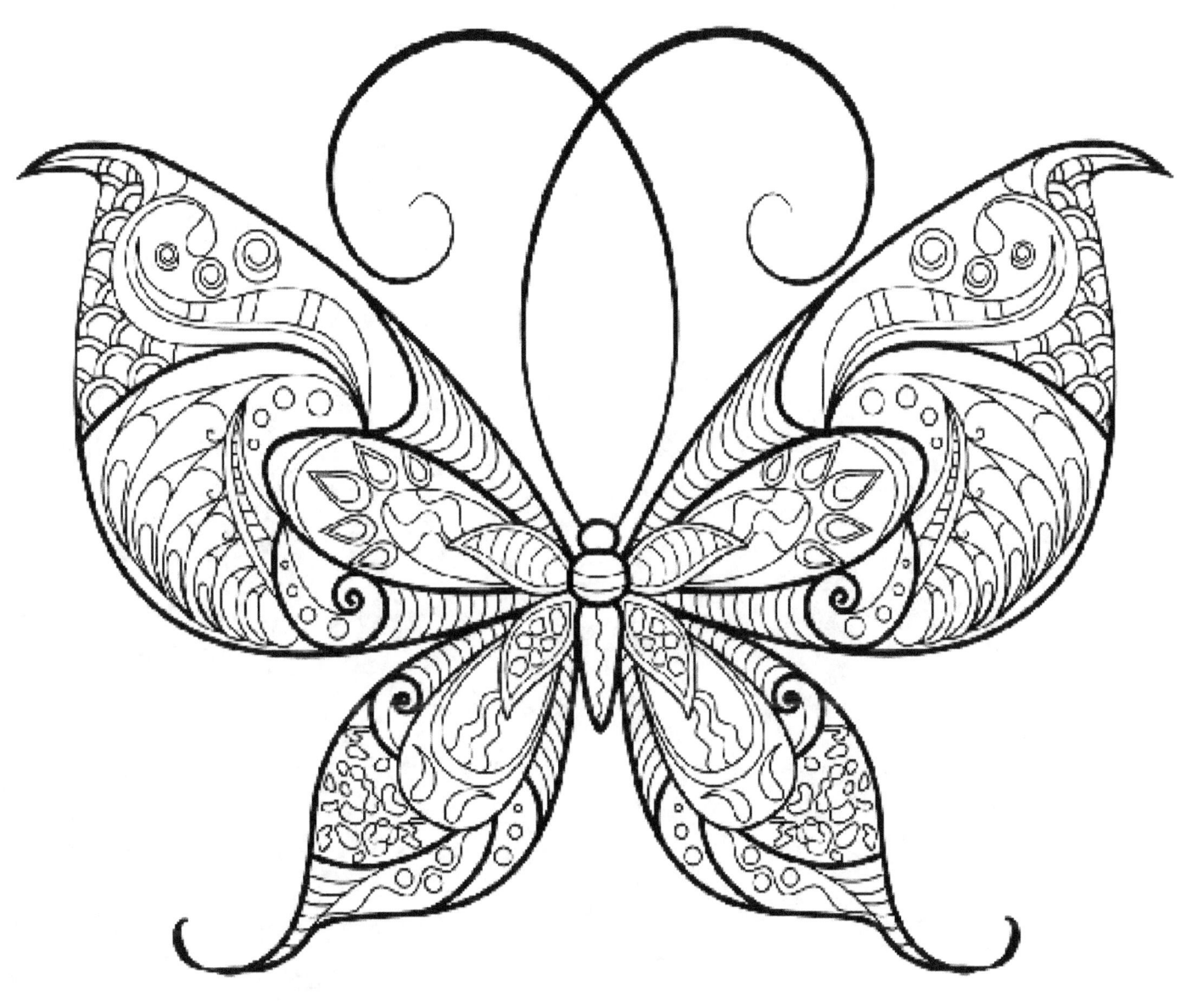

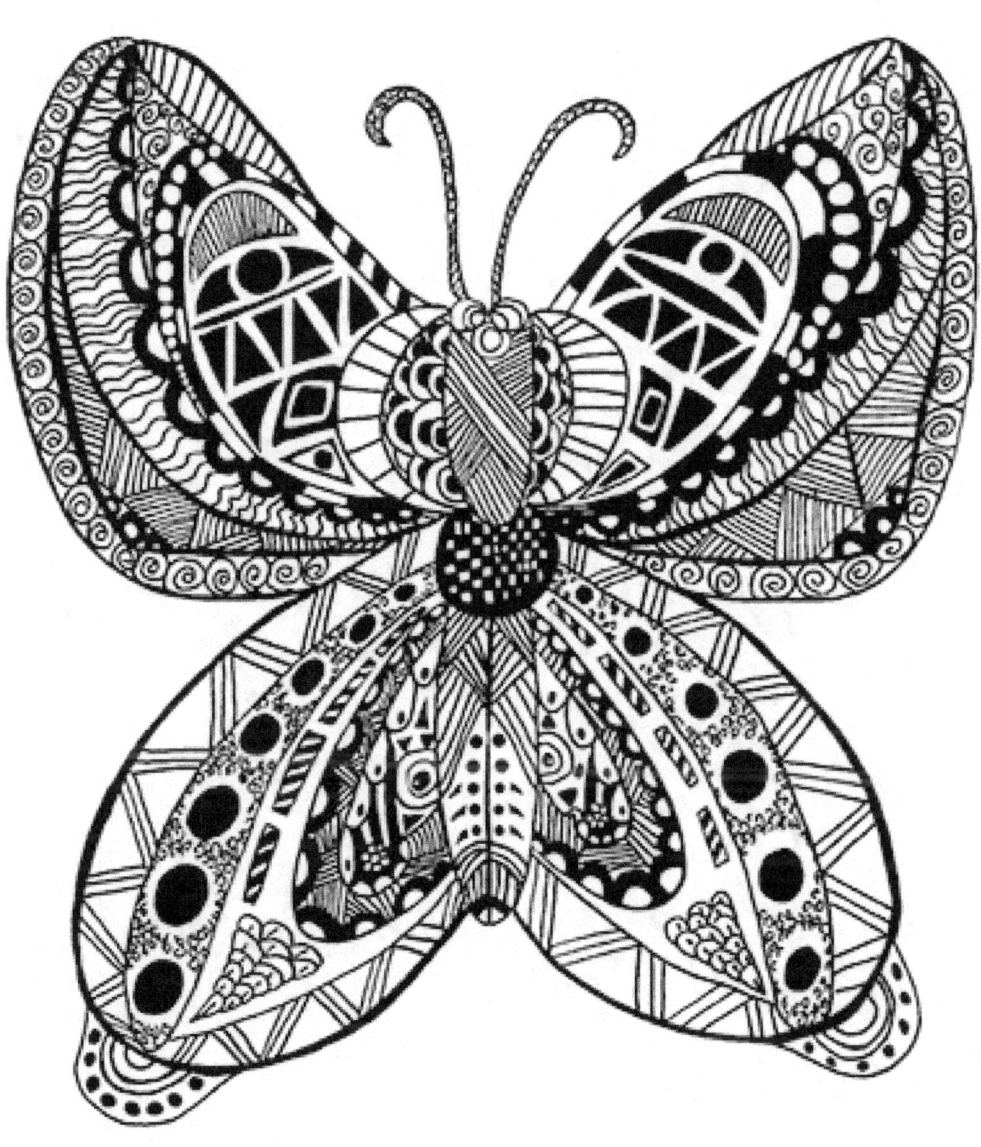

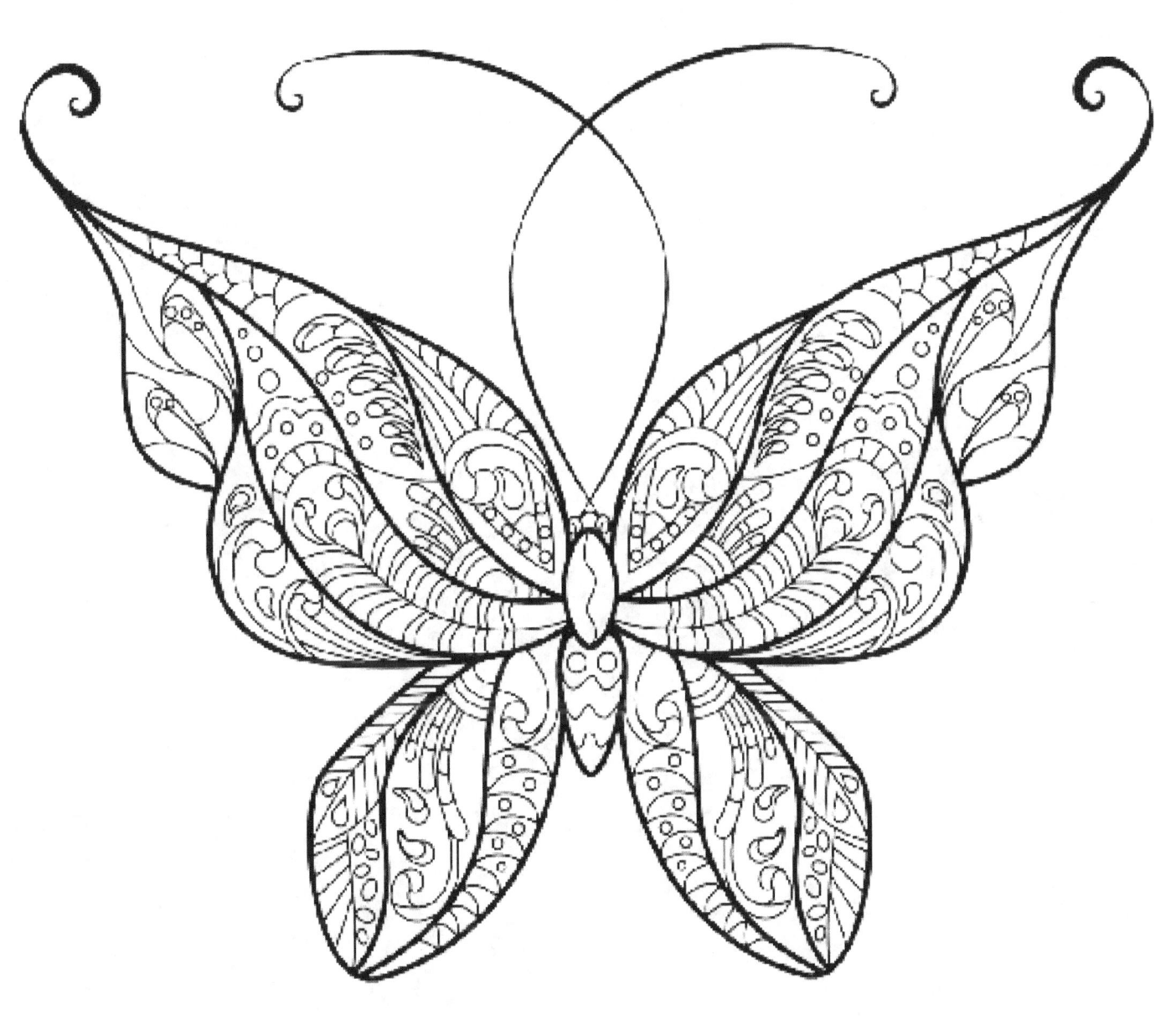

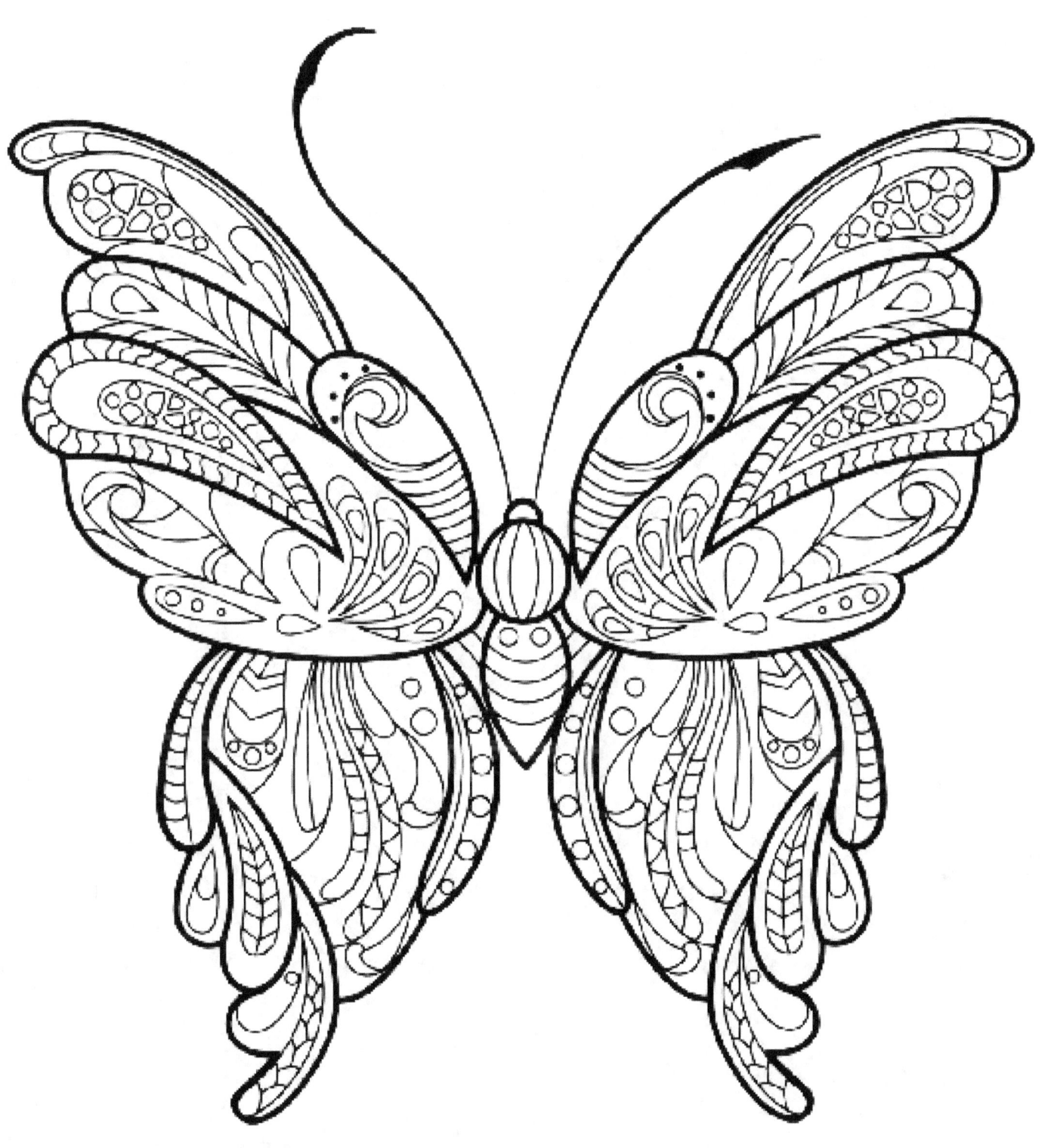

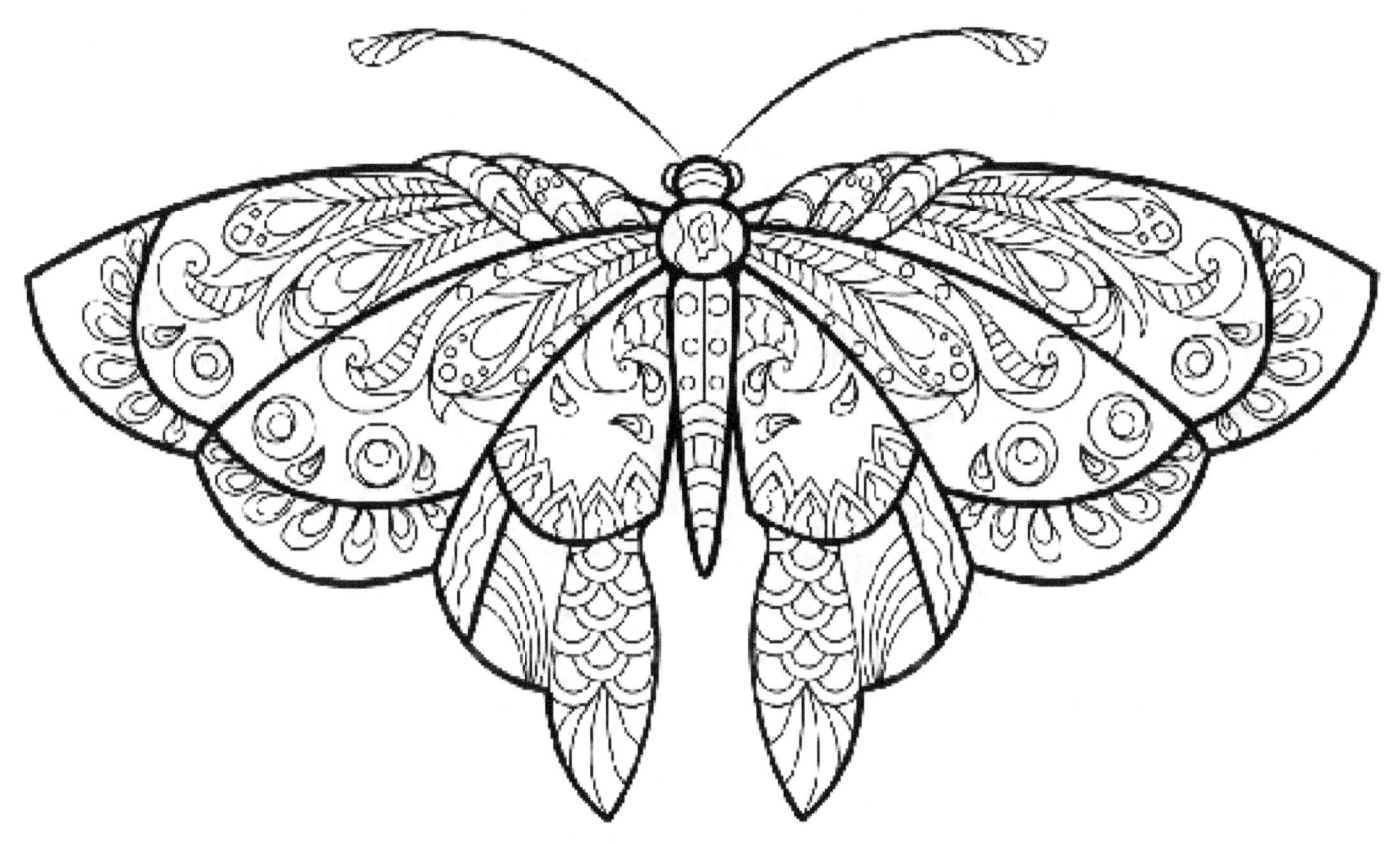